THE

Reapportionment Revolution

Representation, Political Power, and the Supreme Court

STUDIES IN POLITICAL SCIENCE

THE Reapportionment Revolution

Representation, Political Power, and the Supreme Court

BY

GORDON E. BAKER

University of California, Santa Barbara

RANDOM HOUSE

NEW YORK

FIRST PRINTING

Library of Congress Catalog Card Number: 65-13758

Manufactured in the United States of America
by H. Wolff, New York

Portions of this book are
derived from the author's
Rural Versus Urban Political Power,
published in 1955.

For
June
Jeffrey *and* Leslie

Preface

A decade ago, the results of my initial research into the question of legislative representation and apportionment appeared under the title, *Rural Versus Urban Political Power*. That work outlined and analyzed the nature and consequences of unequal representation in state legislatures, with some attention to its effect on national politics. As the title suggests, the study focused on competing urban and rural political interests.

The 1960 federal census revealed a continuing population mobility affecting the representative strength of localities in both state legislatures and in Congress, with preponderant suburban growth adding a new political dimension. The implications of the census were seen in efforts to bring about reapportionments of legislatures, or in some states to amend constitutions in ways which would affect representation. The problem had also attracted the increasing attention of scholars and civic groups, and some lower federal courts had even suggested the need for a re-examination of traditional judicial nonintervention in malapportionment suits.

For all of these reasons, my publishers and I agreed

early in 1962 that a complete revision of the earlier study was needed. Then, on March 26 of that year, the United States Supreme Court signaled its willingness to accept jurisdiction over cases challenging the constitutionality of state legislative apportionments with its decision in the landmark case of *Baker v. Carr*. An ensuing flood of litigation culminated in the Supreme Court's "one man, one vote" decisions of 1964. The period since 1962 has witnessed a judicial revolution entailing widespread political repercussions. In this fresh setting it became increasingly clear that a mere revision of my earlier study would not suffice. While some of its background material has been retained, the present volume is substantially a new work and appears under a title more appropriate to its contemporary focus. Evolving over a period of three years, the manuscript underwent repeated updating and revisions as the subject matter itself changed in swift and kaleidoscopic fashion. In view of this fluid condition, it seemed the better course of wisdom to focus on major characteristics underlying the recent institutional transformations, and their implications for political theory and practice. It is hoped that such a treatment will yield the most enduring study possible under such hazardous circumstances.

Many persons and organizations have provided valuable assistance over a period of years. While specific obligations are reported in the text and notes, others should be mentioned here. I have long been grateful to Richard C. Snyder, of the University of California at Irvine, for providing me with my first opportunity to publish a systematic study of representation. The National Municipal League has been a ready and cooperative source of data and other assistance on countless occasions; thanks go in particular to the League's Senior Associate William J. D. Boyd, a former student and long-time friend. Congressional Quarterly, Inc., has kindly permitted me to draw on essential data from various issues of their *Congressional Quarterly Weekly*

Report and other special publications. Ralph Eisenberg of the University of Virginia contributed timely suggestions and materials that would otherwise have escaped my notice. Finally, I am indebted to Malcolm E. Jewell of the University of Kentucky for critically reading an early draft of the manuscript and for making several helpful suggestions.

I am especially grateful to the Social Science Research Council for the award of a Faculty Research Fellowship in 1962. Grants for travel and clerical assistance by the University of California are also acknowledged.

GORDON E. BAKER

November, 1965
Santa Barbara, Calif.

CONTENTS

THE

Reapportionment Revolution

Representation, Political Power,

and the Supreme Court

CHAPTER 1

Years of Decisions: 1962–1964

On June 15, 1964, the Supreme Court of the United States handed down a group of companion decisions that won immediate recognition as historical landmarks. Judging appeals from lower court decisions affecting six different states, the highest tribunal declared that representation in both houses of state legislatures must be based on population. One week later, the Court handed down similar decisions (without opinions) for nine additional states.

The basis for all fifteen decisions was the holding that the Fourteenth Amendment's equal protection clause guarantees to each citizen representative equality in his state capitol. Speaking for the Court, Chief Justice Earl Warren declared: "Legislators represent people, not trees or acres. Legislators are elected by voters, not farms or cities or economic interests." Basic to a representative form of government such as ours, the opinion continued, is the right of the citizen to cast his vote and to have it counted in full. Any substantial disparity in the population of legislative districts has the same effect as allotting a different number of votes to different individuals. "The weight of a citizen's vote," declared the Chief Justice, "cannot be made to depend on where he lives." [1]

These state legislative apportionment cases emerged from a divided Supreme Court. The Chief Justice spoke for a six-man majority. Two other Justices, Tom C. Clark and Potter Stewart, concurred with the results in some of the cases but not in the others. Taking a more restrictive view of the equal protection clause of the Fourteenth Amendment, they dissented from the majority's reasoning, seeing it as "a long step backward," one that converted a "particular political philosophy into a constitutional rule." [2]

Passionately dissenting in all the cases was Justice John Marshall Harlan, who extemporized from the bench about the "solemnity of this occasion" and warned his brethren that so sweeping a decision could damage the Court's prestige. "In every accurate sense of the term," Justice Harlan declared, these decisions involved "the Court amending the Constitution." [3] In his written dissent, Justice Harlan insisted: "The Constitution is not a panacea for every blot upon the public welfare, nor should this Court, ordained as a judicial body, be thought of as a general haven for reform movements." [4]

These dramatic decisions in June, 1964 culminated a two-year period during which the nation's highest tribunal provided the impetus for an institutional revolution of the deepest significance. The groundwork had been laid on March 26, 1962, when the Supreme Court accepted jurisdiction of an apportionment case. In *Baker v. Carr*,[5] urban plaintiffs in Tennessee had challenged their state legislature's failure, during half a century, to reapportion legislative power in accordance with widespread population shifts. While declining to decide the merits of the controversy, the Court, by a 6 to 2 vote, broke new ground by holding that Federal courts could properly hear lawsuits challenging existing legislative apportionments. Moreover, the high tribunal acknowledged that a pattern of inequalities in district populations might constitute a violation of the Fourteenth Amendment's equal protection of the laws clause.

While legislative apportionment evokes less public concern and reaction than issues involving civil rights and socio-economic problems, it nonetheless portends a change of enormous significance in the governmental power structures of the states. Should judicial stimulus result in lawmaking bodies substantially representative of their publics, it would (and in several states already does) involve a marked shift in political power from rural and small-town areas to urban and suburban communities. In many capitals such a transformation would predictably result in significantly different types of public policy decisions.

The nature of the apportionment pattern had become increasingly clear by 1962, when the Supreme Court opened the doors of Federal courts to suits challenging representative inequality. Since the turn of the century the United States has changed from a country three-fifths rural to a nation over two-thirds urban and suburban. But state legislatures did not reflect this shift, becoming less and less representative of population. Rural dominance was natural and logical in the nineteenth century, as long as the nation was largely agrarian; but the failure of state representative bodies to reflect the changing character of society resulted in a number of problems for a modern industrial age.

In most states, by 1962, citizens living in urban or suburban districts were accorded much less political weight than rural or small-town residents. According to the principle of political equality, all legislators should represent approximately equal numbers of citizens. Yet either because of state constitutional provisions freezing apportionments or because of legislative refusal to redistrict, the average urban constituency had grown considerably more populous than typical rural or small-town districts. For example, a city or suburban representative might speak for upwards of 50,000 persons, while a rural or small-town legislator might represent only 10,000 or 20,000. On a statewide basis, such discrepancies had typically left urban dwellers in a far weaker political position than constituents from the countryside. The result in most states was minority rule by artificially created legislative majorities.

Political Reactions to *Baker v. Carr*

Reactions to the Supreme Court's reapportionment decision in the spring of 1962 were mixed, though most political and newspaper comment appeared to be favorable. Attorney General Robert F. Kennedy hailed the Court's move as "a landmark in the development of representative government." [6] While the Tennessee case was under appeal, the Justice Department, through Solicitor General Archibald Cox, had supported the urban plaintiffs with a brief *amicus curiae*. At his press conference a few days following the announcement of the *Baker* decision, President John F. Kennedy commented: "Quite obviously, the right to fair representation and to have each vote counted equally is, it seems to me, basic to the successful operation of a democracy." He added:

> I would hope that through the normal political processes, these changes to insure equality of voting, equality of representation, would be brought about by the responsible groups involved, in the States, and in the National Government. . . . It's the responsibility of the political groups to respond to the need, but if no relief is forthcoming, then of course it would seem to the administration that the judicial branch must meet a responsibility.[7]

Favorable responses to the reapportionment decision cut across party lines. United States Senator Kenneth Keating, New York Republican, praised the Court's ruling as one that would "meet with the approval of everyone who believes in giving full significance to the equal protection clause of the Fourteenth Amendment."[8] And Senator Barry Goldwater, Arizona Republican, termed the *Baker* case "a proper decision." He added: "I know there are those who say that the conservatives' political strength will be reduced if the cities gain more representation in the legislatures. But I don't agree with that. . . . There are proportionately just as many conservatives in the metropolitan as in the rural areas."[9]

Among critics of the reapportionment decision were several Congressmen from the South, where patterns of legislative representation were among the most vulnerable to attack on grounds of inequality. The leader of the Southern Democratic bloc in the United States Senate, Richard B. Russell of Georgia, charged the Supreme Court with "another major assault on our constitutional system." He continued: "The true protection of our rights as citizens and the cornerstone of our great civilization is founded on the system of checks and balances which the majority of the Supreme Court has set out to destroy."[10] Other southerners, however—especially urban spokesmen—welcomed the news that there was now the possibility of circumventing their own legislatures in seeking representative equality.

In all states there was some apprehension among officials, notably legislators themselves, about the potential implications of the decision in the Tennessee case. This reaction was not necessarily vocal, but typically took the form of watchful waiting. As apportionment lawsuits grew in most states, clashes between defenders and opponents of existing representative patterns took the form of legal briefs. A later reaction had materialized by the end of 1962, when state legislative leaders began a move to amend the Federal Constitution so that apportionment disputes could not be subject to the jurisdiction of Federal courts.

Judicial Repercussions, 1962–1964

In deciding *Baker v. Carr*, the Supreme Court provided no specific standards for lower courts to follow in subsequent apportionment litigation. While the majority explained at some length its reasons for accepting jurisdiction, it did not indicate what kinds of representative patterns would violate the Fourteenth Amendment. Moreover, statements of two members of the majority in particular made it difficult to predict how the high tribunal might decide the merits of future cases. Justice Stewart stressed the narrow scope of the Court's decision, while Justice Clark suggested that a number of highly unequal representative patterns could be reconciled with the equal protection clause, provided they were "rational." In spite of these doubts and ambiguities, the *Baker* decision immediately spawned a rash of apportionment suits in both state and Federal courts. Charles Rhyne, successful counsel for the urban plaintiffs in Tennessee, declared that "*Baker v. Carr* has had an impact like an earthquake. An impact far beyond even [our] most optimistic dreams. . . ." Summarizing the major events in a period of only five months after the Supreme Court's decision, Rhyne elaborated as follows:

> 1. Courts have directly or indirectly invalidated state law or constitutional apportionments of legislatures in whole or in part in 16 states. . . .
> 2. There are over 50 cases pending in 32 states with new cases being reported constantly.
> 3. Over 40 opinions have been rendered and many more orders have been signed by courts.
> 4. Eight legislatures have held special sessions to adopt new laws or proposed constitutional amendments.[11]

These and subsequent developments indicated that the apportionment problem would probably be the major focus of state political and judicial developments for years to come. As early as the elections of 1962 some states had already felt the impact of the new jurisprudence on reapportionment. In both Georgia and Maryland one legislative house was elected under new apportionments, while both houses in Tennessee and Alabama had new districts for the 1962 elections. These were generally regarded as stopgap measures, with the courts usually giving notice that improved apportionment acts were expected from future legislative sessions.

The immediate changes in the political fabric of Georgia were little short of revolutionary. Under judicial prodding to reconstruct at least one house on a population basis before 1963, the state legislature complied by reconstituting the senate. As a result, the most populous county, containing Atlanta, increased its representation from one senator to seven. One of these new senators elected in 1962 was the first Negro legislator in Georgia since Reconstruction. Another consequence of the reapportionment precedent was the invalidation of the state's county unit system, by which statewide officers had been chosen in the Democratic party primary by county unit votes rather than by popular votes. In the August, 1962, primary, the first urban candidate for governor of Georgia in the twentieth century won the nomination (and hence the election). A dramatic example of the impact of the new electoral system was the defeat by popular vote of the veteran Congressman James C. Davis, who would have won under the former unit count.[12]

The wave of apportionment litigation in most of the nation was not characterized by judicial action either so immediate or so vigorous as in the instances just mentioned. Nonetheless, within one year of *Baker v. Carr*, the Congressional Quarterly Service counted lower court decisions on reapportionment in twenty-five states; of these, nineteen legislatures were held to have one or both houses apportioned in violation of the Fourteenth Amendment.[13] Frequently, state and Federal judges allowed a specific period of time in which the legislature was to act, typically retaining jurisdiction in the interim. Also, court decrees were sometimes stayed to allow legislative deliberation. Within that same one-year period, some fifteen states had passed reapportionment acts, with several other states expected to follow suit.[14] Fear of court action apparently underlay much of this legislative activity. Yet most of these reapportionments fell far short of equal representation in both houses, and did not escape the challenge of new litigation.

Since the Supreme Court's 1962 decision on apportionment did not directly confront the substantive issues, it is hardly surprising that the dispositions in lower courts sometimes faced in different and even opposite directions. While generally holding in favor of more equal representative patterns, judges were frequently cautious about the nature and extent of their new responsibilities to hear cases in this field. Among the major uncertainties were the following questions: How equal must districts be? What remedies can courts fashion? Is inequality deriving from a state constitution as vulnerable as inequality growing out of legislative action or inaction? Can either house in a bicameral legislature deviate from a general population pattern, and if so, how much? Should courts decline to interfere whenever political relief (such as the initiative) is available to voters? Are state constitutional apportionments sponsored by popular initiative and approved at the polls as vulnerable to attack as those written by legislatures or conventions? Are congressional as well as state legislative districts subject to judicial scrutiny?

In seeming recognition of the need for resolving many of these issues, the United States Supreme Court announced in June, 1963 that it would hear argument on eight cases (from five states) during its term beginning the following October. These cases involved challenges to legislative apportionment (and in some instances, to judicial disposition) in Alabama, Maryland, New York, and Virginia. Congressional districting patterns were contested in New York and Georgia. After the Court began its term it added appeals from several more states, including a decision invalidating Delaware's legislative districting, as well as a challenge to Colorado's newly enacted apportionment provisions.

Answers to one restricted category of questions came on February 17, 1964, when the Supreme Court disposed of the congressional cases. In *Wesberry v. Sanders*, the high tribunal, dividing 6 to 3, held that "as nearly as is practicable one man's vote in a Congressional election must be worth as much as another's." [15] Population disparities of over three to one among Georgia's districts were held to violate the section of Article I of the Constitution which provides that representatives be chosen "by the People of the several States." The other congressional case decided on that day involved a charge of racial and ethnic gerrymandering of New York City's congressional districts, which were relatively equal in population. With two dissenters, the Supreme Court dismissed the challenge as not having proven that racial considerations motivated the legislature in drawing district lines.[16] And the Court appeared reluctant to intervene in the general area of political gerrymanders.

Since the *Wesberry* decision avoided the question of the Fourteenth Amendment and instead relied upon provisions of Article I for the make-up of the House of Representatives, there was still uncertainty as to how the justices would decide the state cases. The trend of decisions after *Baker v. Carr*, both from the Supreme Court and among lower courts, was unmistakably in the direction of greater representative equality. Even then, the sweeping nature of the state apportionment decisions in June, 1964 surprised many who had anticipated that the trend would continue. It would have been entirely possible for the Supreme Court to have reached the same disposition of all six cases before it, to have declared that all of these particular state provisions violated the requirements of the Fourteenth Amendment, without proceeding to announce at that time a general rule for all states. Indeed, such an approach was urged on the high tribunal by Solicitor General Cox, again appearing as *amicus curiae* for those challenging malapportionments, as he had done earlier in *Baker v. Carr*. But perhaps the Court wanted to articulate ground rules specific enough to serve as a guide to lower courts and avoid conflicting decisions on comparable situations. After announcing its general population standards in the decisions of June 15, the high tribunal applied them one week later in decisions (without opinions) challenging apportionment patterns in the states of Connecticut, Florida, Idaho, Illinois, Iowa, Michigan, Ohio, Oklahoma, and Washington.

Political Repercussions to the 1964 Decisions

The Supreme Court's decisions of June, 1964 stunned and bewildered many political figures and surprised even some who welcomed the rulings. The reactions across the nation varied, of course, but tended to be less favorable than after *Baker v. Carr* in 1962. The reasons are clear enough. Even though the earlier Tennessee case was obviously a judicial landmark, the Court had not decided the merits. Consequently, legislators and other public officials in many states were confident that they would remain unaffected by the Tennessee case due to different circumstances.

In spite of the more adverse climate of opinion in 1964, there were numerous favorable reactions which cut across party lines. Democratic National Chairman John M. Bailey praised the end of "archaic" apportionments, adding that "this is something the Democratic party had long advocated and fought for and certainly welcomes." Republican National Chairman William E. Miller, who was nominated as his party's candidate for

Vice President a month later, announced that the decision was "in the national interest and in the Republican party's interest." [17] Spokesmen for both major parties could legitimately claim particular advantages from reapportionment. While the impact would vary greatly from state to state, Democrats could look for gains in many cities, while Republicans could reap benefits from newly recognized suburban strength.

In the period following the June decisions, some states responded by reapportioning in accordance with court rulings, while others were granted brief delays until after the November elections. Still others were not sufficiently far along in the judicial appeals process to have immediate worries about the problem. But even these could look ahead to the seemingly inevitable, since the Court had laid down rather specific guidelines.

It is not surprising, then, that Congress soon felt pressures from state officials to do something. And many Senators and Representatives were more than willing to take the lead. During the summer of 1964 proposals to amend the United States Constitution in order to circumvent the effect of the apportionment decisions were introduced in both houses of Congress. Other measures attempted to delay reapportionment by exempting such cases from the jurisdiction of the Federal courts. While such moves failed in 1964, the first session of the 89th Congress, convening early in 1965, became the scene of a renewed political battle over a constitutional amendment to allow states to modify the population standard in legislative apportionment.

The fast-moving events seemed destined to confront the nation with some of the most fundamental questions ever raised concerning the American political system. To understand the entire problem in proper perspective, it is necessary to examine the nature of representation in terms of its theoretical development, its institutional operation, and its emerging constitutional status. To these subjects the following chapters are devoted.

CHAPTER 2

Representative Equality in American Thought and Practice

Equality of representation in the lawmaking tax levying bodies is a fundamental requisite of a free government, and no unbiased, fair, or just man has any right to claim a greater share of the voting power of the people than is granted to every other man similarly situated. It is vain for the people to hope for reforms of abuses or righteous results in legislation if the legislative bodies are not fairly representative of all the people, without discrimination.[1]

The above assertion by a state jurist is a concise summation of the theory of equal representation—a theory based upon the moral equality of all persons in a free government. It is usual to think of the principle of equality as a bar against discrimination upon grounds of race, creed, or social class. To these we might add locality. For what can justify allotting an inferior role to citizens merely because they live in certain geographical areas?

One of the basic assumptions of democratic rule is the doctrine of political equality. "One man, one vote" is the most familiar and concise phrase summing up the ideal that all citizens should have approximately the same political weight. The logical correlative, "one vote, one value," means that representative assemblies should reflect as closely as possible the make-up of the body politic. After all, how valuable is equal suffrage if all votes are not weighed equally in a representative context? A logical concomitant of the right to vote is the right to have each vote counted—and counted as a full vote. Any considerable distortion in representative patterns means a dilution of some votes—in effect, a restriction of suffrage.

If we regard equal representation as the logical extension of the ideal of political equality, we might next ask how it is that the prevailing practice deviated so markedly from democratic theory. A brief historical analysis may indicate the development and strength of the egalitarian concept of representation, as well as some reasons for the general failure of American legislatures to embody that theory, prior to the judicially inspired transformations of 1962 and after.

The Development of Equal Representation in England

The concept of political equality under representative government is a relatively recent one. The British House of Commons, the "Mother of Parliaments," had its origins in a feudal rather than a democratic society. At the outset the Commons represented localities rather than individuals. Counties and boroughs sent delegates to deal with the king on behalf of the various communities. The size of the constituency was irrelevant. With the breakdown of feudal society and the eventual emergence of a philosophy more concerned with individualism and eventually with equality, difficulties arose. The older representative pattern persisted in the face of fluid and changing conditions. The result was a "rotten borough" Parliament. The "rotten boroughs" were constituencies that had become insignificant in population and importance, but that continued to be represented as before in Commons. At the same time thriving cities such as Manchester and Birmingham had come into prominence with no representation at all.

Indeed, a few boroughs had even become entirely depopulated, but still had seats in the legislature. A classic example was Old Sarum, with no inhabitants and two representatives, the same number that represented nearly a million persons in Yorkshire. Since no resident requirement existed, "rotten boroughs" still sent members to Parliament. The owners of the land could dispense seats much like patronage, and boroughs were bought, sold, and inherited. By 1793 an estimated eighty-four individuals controlled 157 seats in Commons, while a majority of that body was returned by fewer than 15,000 electors.[2] Not until 1832 were the worst inequalities among districts removed, while a proper urban-rural balance was attained even later. The inception of modern British democracy can be dated from the Great Reform Act of 1832, with its constitutional principle that representation bears a direct relationship to population.

American Ideas and Experience

THE COLONIAL PERIOD. In view of this English background, it is not surprising that representation in colonial America was originally based on localities. The isolated nature of early settlements, plus a high degree of autonomy in local communities and a similarity to each other in their make-up, provided a natural basis for representation by town. Far from being considered as a right, representation in the early colonial period was a duty, often fulfilled with reluctance. In 1670 Virginia levied a fine of 10,000 pounds of tobacco for any county failing to send two burgesses to the assembly. Massachusetts also assessed fines on delinquent towns, and in addition adopted a maximum quota of delegates for any community, "since the expense involved made representation a privilege not greatly desired." [3]

However, the theory of political equality gradually developed. Frontier conditions and isolation from Europe created a much more fertile soil for its growth here than in the England of that time. As colonial unrest grew over the lack of representation in the British Parliament, an internal struggle was also taking place between the older coastal commercial settlements and the rapidly expanding, more democratic frontier groups. The western counties chafed under their inferior political status in the councils of most colonies. Threats of armed violence by frontiersmen in Pennsylvania resulted in provisions for a just apportionment of representatives in that commonwealth's constitution of 1776, which stated that "representation in proportion to the number of taxable inhabitants is the only principle which can at all times secure liberty, and make the voice of a majority of the people the law of the land."

Similar protests arose in other new states. In his *Notes on Virginia*, written during the American Revolution, Thomas Jefferson pointed to two chief defects in his state's constitution. One consisted of restrictions on suffrage. The second: "Among those who share the representation, the shares are very unequal. Thus the county of Warwick, with one-hundred fighting men, has an equal representation with the county of Loudon, which has one thousand seven hundred and forty-six. So that every man in Warwick has as much influence in the government as seventeen in Loudon." [4] Jefferson proposed a model constitution, with legislative representation based on the number of qualified electors.

In some parts of New England the right of every town, regardless of size, to send a delegate to the legislature was brought into question. In 1777 a convention from Essex County declared misrepresentation to be the chief defect in a proposed constitution for Massachusetts. The group issued a document setting forth the democratic ideal of political equality: "The rights of representation should be so equally and impartially distributed, that the representative should have the same views and interests with the people at large. . . . Let the representatives be apportioned among the respective counties, in proportion to their number of freemen."[5]

REVOLUTION AND CONSTITUTION. It is clear that the question of representation took on crucial importance in the revolutionary atmosphere of the later eighteenth century. It is scarcely necessary to note the importance of this issue in the ultimate withdrawal of the thirteen American colonies from the British Empire. The Declaration of Independence stressed democratic ideals of equality and the right of representation. As is often the case, however, political institutions lagged behind the predominant theory of the day, so that political equality was far from complete in practice. All of the new states at the outset restricted suffrage through property qualifications, a situation that helped delay the development of the equitable representative patterns so widely advocated.

When delegates gathered in 1787 to create a new constitution for the United States, the smaller states were reluctant to yield their accustomed equality of status with the large—a status granted as a matter of convenience and necessity under the war-born Articles of Confederation. Yet the democratic ideal of representation as a substitute for direct action of the people was strong. Early in the debates James Wilson announced: "The doctrine of Representation is this—first the representative ought to speak the language of his Constituents, and secondly that his language or vote should have the same influence as though the Constituents gave it."[6] James Madison aded that the states "ought to vote in the same proportion in which their citizens would do, if the people of all the States were collectively met."[7] While this argument had much force, and while the proposal underlying it actually received a favorable vote at one point, it was apparent that no federation would be possible without a concession to the small states. As a result, the principle of direct representation was modified by the creation of a senate with equal membership from the constituent states. In the *Federalist* papers Madison attempted to anticipate possible objections to the equal representation of states in the Senate by emphasizing that the arrangement was a result of concession and necessity rather than principle. It was also, he added, a recognition of the portion of sovereignty remaining in the states, since the new nation would be a "compound republic," as contrasted with a single incorporated nation, which would necessarily provide a proportionate share for every district.[8] Madison here assumes an acceptance of the proportionate principle *within* unitary republics, such as the states themselves.

NEW STATES AND NEW PROBLEMS. Settlement of the question of representation on the Federal level did not end the struggle over the problem in America. Within the various states, controversy persisted between the democratic frontier elements and the tidewater aristocracy, factions that had temporarily been united under the popular banners of the Revolution. The rapidly growing western sections felt that they were being exploited by the older and wealthier eastern areas, especially in regard to discriminatory and harsh taxation. It was not surprising that the interior should blame the twin obstacles of restricted suffrage and inequitable representation in the legislatures.[9]

As new states (such as Kentucky and Tennessee) were formed along the frontier, their constitutions reflected some of this popular ferment. Also embodying the democratic theory of representation was the Northwest Ordinance of 1787, which provided the framework for the future organization of government in the vast region beyond the Appalachian Mountains. The importance attached to the subject of representation is revealed in the

Ordinance's stipulation that "the inhabitants of the said territory shall always be entitled to the benefits of the writs of habeas corpus and of the trial by jury, of a proportionate representation of the people in the legislature, and of judicial proceedings according to the course of the common law."[10] Moreover, as the nation moved westward during the nineteenth century, congressional statutes establishing new territories usually contained similar provisos of equal representation.

In the older states the period from 1820 to 1840 witnessed a rapid extension of popular power, as one constitution after another underwent revision. While the struggle for political equality centered primarily on suffrage restrictions, it often involved the question of representation as well, since conservatives generally sought to retain at least an upper house representing the propertied interests. State after state, however, yielded to the advance of democracy; property qualifications were abandoned and white manhood suffrage was largely achieved by the 1830's. In regard to representation, the trend in newly formed states definitely reflected the democratic ideal of an equal population standard, as can readily be seen in the provisions of state constitutions as they were first written. Six of the original thirteen states provided that both houses be based on population (or with only a slight modification in one house). And, of the remaining thirty-seven states, the constitutions of all but seven originally invoked a similar standard.[11] Some states, especially those with large land area and few inhabitants, took account of territory as well as people, but the inclusion of such units as counties and towns often made little practical difference. Frontier conditions of isolation and poor communications provided a rationale for the representation of every political unit. Also, as a simple convenience, counties were sometimes given a minimum representation in the legislature. These deviations seemed to do little violence to the population principle when the distribution of a state's inhabitants was fairly equal and the number of counties comparatively few.[12]

A stress on localities persisted in some older states, especially in New England, but even here the traditional pre-Revolutionary practice of town representation was challenged. A successful fight for a change in the historic pattern took place in Massachusetts, where small-town dominance evoked controversy at the state constitutional convention of 1853. There Charles Francis Adams contended: "I maintain that the moment a majority in a republic assumes to draw a distinction with the intent that certain men shall be enabled to enjoy twice or thrice the amount of political power which an equal number of other men are to possess, that is the hour when tyranny begins." [13] Within a few years the theory enunciated by Adams prevailed and the equal district system replaced town representation.

Toward the end of the nineteenth century a distrust of growing cities resulted in restrictions on urban power. This indicated a reversal of the late eighteenth-century condition of underrepresented frontier and agrarian areas. One explanation for this curious turnabout is that threats to the status quo had largely shifted from rural to urban groups. The rise of cities in the nineteenth century spawned the growth of a large laboring class, whose voting power alarmed men of substance, both rural and urban. With the earlier battles over an extended suffrage already lost, conservatives of a later generation sought to neutralize its effects in a number of states by controlling the apportionment of legislative representation. These restrictions were facilitated by the widespread exposure of bossism, graft, and corruption in many big cities, conditions which created some understandable popular distrust of urban political power.

An emphasis on localities, together with the failure of lawmaking bodies to reapportion seats according to population shifts, have always resulted in distortions of democratic standards. In an earlier day of relative simplicity and homogeneity, these discrepancies were less significant. But in an era of phenomenal population changes, the gap between theory and practice had become especially wide. By the middle of the twentieth century the pattern of state legislative representation revealed sharp disadvantages to growing urban and suburban areas, while declining rural districts enjoyed a political power based on an importance long since gone. While no examples in any state quite matched the notoriety of England's Old Sarum, many were not far removed. The term "rotten boroughs," which originally referred to a feudal anachronism, had become an increasingly apt descriptive term for many American state electoral districts.

CHAPTER 3

Representation at the State Level

By the time of the Supreme Court's assumption of jurisdiction over reapportionment cases in March, 1962, inequality of legislative representation was solidly entrenched in all but a handful of the fifty states. Most urban and suburban areas held considerably less than their proportionate share of strength in at least one house of their state legislature, and in many cases in both houses.

The situation had grown increasingly severe with the passage of time. Late in 1961 Professors Paul David and Ralph Eisenberg published a comprehensive study of the twentieth-century changes in the relative representative power patterns within all states. For purposes of comparison, this analysis computed 100 percent as the strength of a vote if all persons—urban, suburban, and rural—had the same representation in their legislatures. The increasing gap in average voting power throughout all fifty states from 1910 through 1960 is revealed in the nationwide percentage figures shown in Table 1.

These findings indicate that by 1960 voters in the largest urban and suburban areas had, on a national average, less than one-half the representation held by

TABLE 1

Relative Values of Representative Strength in State Legislatures: National Averages for All Fifty States

Categories of Counties by Population Size	*1910*	*1930*	*1950*	*1960*
Under 25,000	110	131	141	171
25,000 to 99,999	103	109	114	100
100,000 to 499,999	91	84	83	81
500,000 and over	81	74	78	76

SOURCE: Paul T. David and Ralph Eisenberg, *Devaluation of the Urban and Suburban Vote* (Charlottesville, Va.: Bureau of Public Administration, University of Virginia, 1961), Vol. I, 9. Percentages for 1910, 1930, and 1950 refer to the situation after respective redistrictings, while those for 1960 were necessarily prior to any post-1960 reapportionments and thus indicate the impact of population shifts only. For a follow-up on averages after redistricting in twenty-five states by 1962, see Table 2. (The Bureau has now become the Institute of Government.)

those living in the least populous areas. Moreover, increasing numbers of people were adversely affected as the most underrepresented category grew in importance. While counties of over 500,000 contained 16 percent of the nation's population in 1910, the portion had grown to 37 percent by 1960. As later tables will indicate, the disparities of representative strength in many states are far greater than the total averages in Table 1 imply. If anything, the national statistics in this table give an impression of more moderate inequalities than actually existed.[1]

Reasons for Unbalanced Representation

This increasingly serious degree and extent of representative inequality, as well as judicial recognition of its constitutional status, can be better understood if the reasons explaining the situation are outlined. Because the entire matter is currently in a state of flux, most of the data in this section will present the general picture as it existed in 1962 before judicial intervention increasingly resulted in such a drastic reshuffling of constituencies in so many states. The past tense will therefore ordinarily be employed as a precaution, even though many of the patterns discussed still exist in 1965 and are likely to prevail in at least the near future. Whenever possible, however, significant changes occurring between the 1962 and 1964 apportionment decisions will be noted.

The two major causes of unequal representation have been restrictive constitutional provisions and legislative failure to reapportion seats in accordance with population shifts. The first is illustrated by a number of state constitutions calling for representation of area or political subunits regardless of population. Such provisions have taken a variety of forms. Extreme cases were the town representation provisions for the lower houses of the legislatures in Vermont and Connecticut. In the latter state, Hartford's 162,178 residents sent two representatives, as did the town of Union, with a population of only 383. In fact, in 1962 Connecticut's four most populous cities (Hartford, Bridgeport, New Haven, and Waterbury), with a combined population of 578,104, elected only eight members to a lower house of 294. This same share of legislative strength at the small-town end of the scale represented only 3,312 persons. In Vermont, 24 inhabitants of the town of Stratton enjoyed the same share of the lower house as Burlington's 35,531.

Similar distortions were evident in the seven states (New Jersey, Idaho, South Carolina, Montana, New Mexico, Arizona, and Nevada) that allowed each county, large or small, the same weight in the state senate. California modified this arrangement only slightly by combining some of the least populous counties into senate districts. Some resulting deviations from democratic theory could be seen in these examples:

Rural Sussex County's 49,255 inhabitants, and metropolitan Essex County's 923,545 each sent one senator to the New Jersey legislature.

Los Angeles County's 6,038,771 people received the same senate representation as 14,196 in the senate district composed of Mono, Inyo, and Alpine counties in the Sierra Nevada mountains.

Other frequent methods of limiting larger urban areas were formulas and ratios that allowed progressively less representation to more populous communities; provisions against dividing counties into districts; minimum representation for each county; maximum limits for populous counties and cities. For instance, Iowa's constitution ensured a double advantage to rural areas by limiting each county to a single senator and by guaranteeing a representative to each of the state's 99 counties, regardless of size. Since the lower house was limited to 108 seats, the restrictive ceiling on the nine most populous counties is obvious.

In a number of cases state constitutional barriers were an accidental remnant from apparently convenient arrangements in the eighteenth and nineteenth centuries, established before the growth of urban centers resulted in an increasingly undemocratic situation. In an earlier day when population was spread less unevenly and the total number of counties in a state remained fairly small, provisions for minimum representation could be justified. Later on, however, shrewd politicians in some states found a convenient advantage in creating many additional counties as a means of increasing legislative strength. Also, special limitations on the growing populous areas became frequent as rural forces in many states modified constitutions while they could still command a majority.

The effects of both casual deviations in the early nineteenth century and the deliberate ones of a later period have been felt with multiplied force in this century. Kansas furnishes an example of the effects of time on the substance of legislative representation. After having a population basis for both houses while still a territory, Kansas provided in its state constitution of 1861 that each county have at least one representative, with the remaining members distributed according to population. Since the constitution provided for a house of 75 to 100 members and Kansas had only 34 counties, population was still the primary factor. But by the time the western part of the state became organized there were 105 counties and a constitutional maximum of 125 representatives. The relative share of seats held by the more populous areas declined sharply.[2] After the 1960 census Kansas' four largest urban counties contained over 37 percent of the population but were limited to 10 percent of the lower house.

In other states the most populous communities were restricted by provisions stating that no county may have more than one senator. These two methods—minimum guarantees for each county and maximum limits for populous areas—reflect two interrelated attitudes about representation, views held especially in rural areas. One is the force of localism, the view that every community should have an equal, or at least a distinct and substantial, voice in the state legislature. That such political units as counties actually denote real communities is assumed rather than proved. The other attitude is the distrust of population centers and the consequent desire to dilute their political strength.

As a result, by 1963 there were only nine states with no constitutional restrictions of any consequence upon a fully democratic pattern of population representation in both houses: Washington, Oregon, South Dakota, Minnesota, Wisconsin, Indiana, Virginia, Massachusetts, and Kentucky. This does not mean, of course, that legislatures in all of these states followed the constitutional stipulations. In several additional states restrictions on equal districting were reasonably moderate in their overall effect. But in any case, it is clear that the major source of representative inequality had become restrictive constitutional provisions. And the trend away from earlier standards of population equality continued. For example, North Dakota abandoned the population basis for one house in 1960, while two years later Colorado followed suit and Nebraska added a geographic consideration to the apportionment provisions for its unicameral legislature.

A second—though less extensive—cause of unrepresentative state legislatures has been the common failure of the lawmaking bodies to keep districting arrangements abreast of population changes. Most state constitutions have long called for periodic reapportionment of one or both houses, usually after every Federal census —provisions that have typically gone unobserved and unenforced. Framers of state constitutions usually attempted to insure that representation would keep pace with future population shifts, but from the hindsight of later experience, we might regard as either optimistic or naive the delegation of such a function to the very body affected by the change. But this is understandable enough. In the rural and small-town society of the nineteenth century, legislative apportionment seemed to pose no crucial problem. While the young nation was expanding westward, state legislatures could avoid major political frictions by simply adding more legislative seats to accommodate increases in both population and territory. Generally it was not until the frontier was closed and urban growth became a significant factor, in the twentieth century, that state after state began to turn aside from the redistricting duty. This negative reaction was accompanied by positive movements in several states to amend constitutions so as to limit and condition the extent of any future reapportionment. As a result, representative inequality in many states was the result of *both* constitutional restrictions and legislative failure to redistrict.

The reasons for such widespread failure of legislatures to live up to state constitutional requirements are not difficult to find. In almost any reapportionment a number of legislators would be personally affected through the abolition or consolidation of districts. A legislator naturally finds the status quo under which he was elected to be satisfactory and usually dreads the prospect of a new and unknown constituency. Also, many refuse to move because their particular party or section would lose strength. Lawmakers from areas of declining population resist the idea of losing seats to growing areas, an attitude typically expressed in a hostility by representatives of smaller communities toward growing cities and suburbs. Finally, interest groups benefiting from the status quo have fought reapportionment.

It should be emphasized that while opposition to reapportionment is more frequent and emphatic among rural legislators, it is shared to a remarkable degree by many of their urban colleagues. While urban areas have consistently outgained rural regions in population, these gains do not occur evenly in and around the cities. In the past decade or two in particular, many of the older, established central city areas have declined in importance and population, yielding to other city territory formerly sparsely settled, particularly to mushrooming suburban growth. Even legislators from expanding areas often resist the addition of more seats, since they do not wish to share power and patronage with others.

One consequence of growing resistance during the twentieth century to periodic reapportionment on a population basis was the widespread adoption of "compromise" plans, which retained a population basis for one house while the second chamber represented or stressed geographic areas. In some states these compromises resulted from stalemates caused by long periods of legislative refusal to honor existing constitutional standards of representative equality. Urban forces yielded their claims to proportionate legislative power by accepting a guarantee of periodic reapportionment in one house, at the price of reduced relative strength in the other. A good example is Illinois, where voters in Chicago accepted a 1954 amendment apportioning one house on population but placing permanent control of the state senate in the downstate region.

The most extreme form of political compromise could be found in states purporting to emulate the United States Congress with a "federal plan." Here it was insisted that since the national Senate represents political units equally, state legislatures can or should parallel the arrangement in their own structure. For example, New Mexico in 1949, Nevada in 1950, and Arizona in 1953 all changed their constitutions to allow each county (most of them sparsely settled) the same weight in the state senate. Other states with similar patterns were Idaho, Montana, New Jersey, and South Carolina, while Vermont merely reversed the order, with a senate based on population and the lower house representing each town equally. In addition to these eight states, a few others, such as California, have used the term "Federal Plan" more loosely to refer to one house based largely, though not entirely, on political units.

While this federal analogy has gained a remarkably uncritical acceptance, even by some in states not employing it, there are several serious flaws in its rationale. For one thing, counties are merely legal agents created by states for administrative purposes. All states are unitary rather than federal in internal make-up. As Karl Bosworth has perceptively observed, "Any 'sovereignty' of counties or towns is based on entrenched political power, not on constitutional or democratic theory." [3] Moreover, counties seldom denote distinct communities of interest. In fact, there are numerous counties in many states that scarcely have any realistic justification for separate existence, much less equal representation. Finally, the structure of the federal prototype, the United States Congress, was the result of an expedient and necessary compromise in 1787 (without which there would have been no union of states) rather than the embodiment of some abstract "principle" of government, as is so frequently asserted.[4]

A broader concept of bicameralism with a more persuasive foundation than the federal analogy is one resting on the principle of checks and balances. Two houses, it is argued, are desirable as a check on each other; furthermore, to check most effectively, they should have different bases of representation. Bicameralism would have no purpose, the argument continues, if both houses represented population, for the second house would then be a mirror of the first and hence redundant. Yet these propositions, too, are open to serious question. For one thing, bicameralism has traditionally served the goal of checks and balances quite apart from the added check of differently based legislative houses. The latter often compounds the internal checks to the point of stalemate. "Nor is it true," one group of scholars has commented, "that two houses based on population will be mirror images of each other. They will, rather, present different reflections or combinations of the various elements that make up the population."[5] Disparities in size, prestige, length of terms, and types of districts typically produce houses of distinct character. Past experience in those states that have had two houses based essentially on population (e.g., Massachusetts, Washington, Oregon) suggests that differences in political outlook can and do occur.

Extent of Unbalanced Representation

The above reasons, then, have contributed to the situation of widespread disparities that characterized most state legislative districts by the time of the Supreme Court's landmark decision in *Baker v. Carr*. By then a variety of ways had been developed to ascertain the representativeness of a lawmaking body on a population basis. The most dramatic and concise way of stressing inequalities is to compare the range of district sizes for any legislative body, which yields a ratio of largest to smallest population per member. While this method has some advantages, it also emphasizes extreme cases that are usually not typical of many other districts. Another approach which more adequately reveals the overall situation is to compute the minimum percentage of the state's population required to elect a majority of a given legislative body. This is done by counting legislators, starting with the least populous districts, until a simple majority of the whole membership is reached. This does not suggest that representatives from these least populous districts would necessarily vote the same way. It is nevertheless a theoretical concept that tells us how narrow a base is possible for a legislative majority and thus suggests a general idea of the average of inequality. This method was applied to the legislative houses in all states in 1955 by Manning J. Dauer and Robert G. Kelsay,[6] and has been used since the 1960 census by the National Municipal League in its publication, *Compendium on Legislative Apportionment.* In 1962 this survey of all fifty states pointed up the extent and intensity of representative inequality throughout the nation. Some of the leading situations found can be summarized as follows: [7]

In only six states were both houses of the legislature apportioned so that at least 40 percent of the state's population was needed to elect a majority of each. Easily leading all states in the degree of representativeness was Oregon, where a majority of legislators from the smallest districts of each house still represented approximately 48 percent of the people. Following in order were Massachusetts, New Hampshire, West Virginia, Wisconsin, and Maine.

Only twenty states had even one house where it required at least 40 percent of the people to elect a legislative majority.

In thirteen states, one third of the population *or less* could elect a majority of *both* houses of the legislature.

Examples of the more spectacular disparities within individual states include the following (all as of 1962):

Nevada's senate had a "theoretical control" figure of only 8 percent of the people, while the corresponding portion in California was 10.7. The least representative lower houses were those of Vermont, Florida, and Connecticut—in each of which only 12 percent or less of the population could elect a majority. Taking both houses into consideration, the state ranking lowest in terms of composite representativeness was Florida, where only 12 percent of the people in the most sparsely settled areas could control a majority of the entire legislature.

While this Dauer-Kelsay scale is probably the most easily understood index [8] of the general representative character of legislative bodies, its figures cannot reveal the nature of those districts having the most inflated power. It is widely recognized that rural areas have been generally overrepresented and urban and suburban districts disadvantaged in terms of legislative strength, but a different method is needed to reveal the precise nature of the situation. The statistical work done in 1961 by Professors David and Eisenberg (summarized briefly at the beginning of this chapter) accomplished this by looking directly at the individual voter, computing the average value of the vote by categories of county population. This method not only indicated the relative value of the vote in communities of varying kinds, but charted the comparative values over a period of years. The David-Eisenberg method used four groupings of county size: under 25,000; 25,000 to 99,999; 100,000 to 499,999; and 500,000 and over. By taking 100 percent as an average base figure, the relative share of the population in each category could be computed for each house and for any particular census year. Thus if a county (or class of counties) had three fourths of its actual population weight in legislative strength, it would have a value of 75; a group of counties overrepresented by one half again the weight of their population would have a composite value of 150. This comprehensive study computed such figures for each house of every state legislature, beginning in 1910.

Table 2 presents a general summary of the relative

TABLE 2

Relative Values of Representative Strength in State Legislatures: Smallest and Largest Categories of Counties, as Percentages of Each Statewide Average, by States, 1910, 1930, 1950, 1960, and 1962 (Partial)

State	1910 S	1910 L	1930 S	1930 L	1950 S	1950 L	1960 S	1960 L	1962 S	1962 L
Alabama	104	45	146	37	194	26	216	25		
Alaska	—	—	—	—	—	—	163	51	142	68
Arizona	109	82	126	68	217	64	533	53		
Arkansas	106	90	109	85	104	81	123	61	123	72
California	119	91	333	48	419	59	562	63	547	65
Colorado	130	72	123	70	141	78	211	70		
Connecticut	169	77	239	79	230	75	216	75		
Delaware	148	69	179	62	186	61	187	61		
Florida	129	47	177	29	276	36	476	16		
Georgia	116	24	129	21	153	29	182	12	181	12
Hawaii	—	—	—	—	—	—	228	67		
Idaho	98	54	119	53	137	46	167	48	162	52
Illinois	112	87	151	71	131	89	151	91		
Indiana	89	111	108	85	120	85	133	69		
Iowa	116	39	128	35	139	40	150	36	147	36
Kansas	115	42	125	34	142	33	176	30		
Kentucky	108	81	126	68	122	76	131	60		
Louisiana	104	105	129	88	158	95	177	105	173	103
Maine	113	94	122	83	127	83	133	81	128	86
Maryland	220	45	260	52	334	62	445	83		
Massachusetts	262	102	273	96	273	100	277	102	277	102

Michigan	113	79	200	55	179	72	205	74		
Minnesota	111	86	124	68	136	60	156	55	134	79
Mississippi	108	92	119	84	129	49	139	34		
Missouri	130	70	154	67	151	73	174	69	167	73
Montana	115	51	114	54	128	56	146	53	145	55
Nebraska	108	55	103	96	115	77	130	66		
Nevada	100	100	122	48	192	43	287	28	255	43
New Hampshire	102	97	102	98	133	98	147	99	147	91
New Jersey	397	60	255	61	253	69	356	76	356	69
New Mexico	100	100	108	62	151	40	237	30		
New York	216	77	303	80	319	84	348	86		
North Carolina	116	89	145	67	173	67	204	61	204	62
North Dakota	101	98	103	90	111	71	122	60	117	69
Ohio	144	85	177	85	204	86	242	87	242	89
Oklahoma	102	98	121	54	150	35	175	27	176	27
Oregon	121	66	139	65	127	86	137	85	109	93
Pennsylvania	192	89	252	88	246	88	317	85		
Rhode Island	263	70	199	73	154	80	154	88	150	88
South Carolina	136	92	154	65	185	65	215	59	215	62
South Dakota	100	102	101	99	105	82	113	66	112	68
Tennessee	97	95	115	70	137	60	162	49		
Texas	94	82	104	70	126	49	156	45	142	51
Utah	124	70	130	82	173	71	232	68		
Vermont	127	89	132	88	132	84	149	83		
Virginia	108	81	109	87	112	89	124	73	120	77
Washington	135	85	128	93	130	94	141	88		
West Virginia	103	97	115	81	130	78	130	69		
Wisconsin	115	100	130	84	104	96	119	92		
Wyoming	100	100	103	76	113	67	132	55		

SOURCE: David and Eisenberg, *op. cit.*, p. 15, plus updated figures furnished by these authors.

values over a period of many years in each state (here using only the most- and least-populous county categories). Both houses of a legislature were averaged to produce a combined figure for this concise scale. The table clearly reveals the steady dilution of the value of the vote in most state legislatures for the counties in the largest population category. Only in a few states—New York, New Jersey, Rhode Island, and, to a small extent, Ohio—did there occur a consistent improvement in the value of the vote in the largest category. In some cases, such as New York, both the largest and smallest population categories improved their positions (with the smallest increasing its degree of overrepresentation), usually indicating some decline in the position of one of the middle categories. In some urban states the improvement in the position of the most populous counties by 1962 is explained largely by suburban growth, which has frequently involved a tapering off of city population and a consequent lessening in its degree of underrepresentation. In other cases, metropolitan growth spilled over into adjoining counties, resulting in a lower value of the legislative vote in the next lower category of counties.

In spite of these few instances, the pattern revealed in the table is obvious and striking. The relative value of the vote in the largest category of population was far less than that of those living in the least populated group; moreover, the disparities between them grew decade by decade until ratios that were modest in many states a half century ago became striking. Of all the states, only two (Massachusetts and Louisiana) showed any legislative *over*representation of those living in the most populous counties, and here it was slight. In these states one or more of the middle categories had some degree of devalued representation.

The final column in Table 2 shows figures for those twenty-five states that accomplished some reapportionment or redistricting after the 1960 census and before

March 26, 1962, when the Supreme Court announced its decision in *Baker v. Carr*. Statistics for the 1960 column reflect the new 1960 census figures applied to the existing districts fixed by prior apportionments (while the three prior columns refer to the situation regarding any reapportionments during the decade noted). Thus the last two columns show the kinds of changes effected by post-1960 redistricting where it had occurred. In general the changes were modest. Most states showed some improvement in the position of their most populous categories, but not enough to invalidate the generalizations made so far. A few states did manage to narrow substantially the disparities between the largest and smallest categories, Oregon, Minnesota, and Alaska being the best examples.[9] In two states (New Hampshire and New Jersey) a regression in the status of the most populous category resulted from reapportionments of a single house in which urban areas had previously become slightly overrepresented (partially offsetting underrepresentation in the other branch) according to the formulas used. The states previously mentioned as ranking highest on the Dauer-Kelsay scale also showed the smallest degrees of inequality among categories in the David-Eisenberg analysis. Oregon again led the states in degree of representative character. It should also be noted that the statistics for the smallest category in Massachusetts and New Hampshire are misleading unless one realizes that this group consists of only a single small county in the latter case and only two counties (with a total population of less than 10,000) in the former. If these are excluded as isolated deviations with slight effect on the overall result, the other categories show a close valuation.

On a nationwide basis, the redistrictings made between the 1960 census and the 1962 Supreme Court apportionment decision produced only minimal shifts that did not materially disturb the general situation of inflated rural power and consequent urban underrepresentation. One reason for this is the fact that in the period mentioned only half of all the states had created new district patterns. Moreover, of these twenty-five reapportionments, only seven affected both legislative chambers. Finally, many of the adjustments in representative power were minor in nature. Table 3 indicates the effects of the post-1960 reapportionments on a national basis.

TABLE 3

Relative Value of Representative Strength in State Legislatures Before and After 1960–1962 Reapportionments

Categories of Counties by Population Size	*1950 Census*	*1960 Census*	*After Reapportionments in 25 States to March 26, 1962*
Under 25,000	141	171	168
25,000 to 99,999	114	123	121
100,000 to 499,999	83	81	83
500,000 and over	78	76	77

SOURCE: Ralph Eisenberg, "Power of Rural Vote," *National Civic Review*, LI (October, 1962), 490.

After the reapportionment decision of March 26, 1962, however, several states hastened to make adjustments in at least one house, usually under judicial prodding. While many of these shifts were stopgaps or were under appeal in the courts, they indicated significant shifts in political power. The aftermath of the *Baker v. Carr* decision demonstrated clearly the impact of even modest judicial involvement as compared with the minimal changes noted prior to 1962 when legislatures felt no potential judicial pressure. Table 4 reveals the extent of shifts in representative patterns in the period between the 1962 and 1964 reapportionment decisions. For this purpose the Dauer-Kelsay index indicates the comparative theoretical control percentages for these years. Exactly half of the states made districting changes of some significance, in many cases dramatic ones.

Far more extensive reapportionments have taken place since the Supreme Court's 1964 decision announcing the one man, one vote rule. The speed of these actions as

TABLE 4

States Making Significant Changes in Legislative Representation in Period Between 1962 and 1964 Supreme Court Apportionment Decisions

(Figures indicate the smallest percentage of a state's population which could elect a majority in each legislative house. The lower the percentage, the less representative of population is the apportionment.)

State	*March 26, 1962* Senate	*March 26, 1962* Lower House	*June 15, 1964* Senate	*June 15, 1964* Lower House
Alabama	25.1	25.7	27.6	37.9
Alaska	35.0	49.0	41.9	47.3
Colorado	29.8	32.1	33.0	45.1
Florida	12.3	14.7	15.2	29.7
Georgia	22.6	22.2	48.3	22.2
Indiana	40.4	34.8	40.5	47.6
Iowa	35.2	26.9	38.9	44.8
Kansas	26.8	18.5	47.8	19.4
Kentucky	42.0	34.1	46.6	44.8
Maryland	14.2	25.3	14.2	35.6
Michigan	29.0	44.0	41.3	46.4
Mississippi	34.6	29.1	37.2	41.2
Montana	16.1	36.6	16.1	40.8
Nebraska	36.6	—	43.9	—
New Mexico	14.0	27.0	14.0	42.0
New York	36.9	38.2	41.8	34.7
North Carolina	36.9	27.1	47.6	27.1
Ohio	41.0	30.3	44.8	29.4
Oklahoma	24.5	29.5	44.5	32.5
Pennsylvania	33.1	37.7	43.4	42.7
Tennessee	26.9	28.7	44.5	39.7
Virginia	37.7	36.8	41.1	40.5
West Virginia	46.7	40.0	46.7	46.2
Wisconsin	45.0	40.0	48.4	45.4
Wyoming	26.9	35.8	24.1	46.5

SOURCE: National Municipal League.

well as the number of states involved comprise an institutional revolution unmatched in American history. By mid-summer of 1965, thirty-four states had completed actions, some of which were awaiting either challenges or final court review. Another eleven states were in the process of working out apportionment patterns. The accompanying map reveals the nationwide status of apportionment as of early August, 1965. By the end of the year, several additional states had completed action, while none of the remainder had escaped the filing of suits challenging existing legislative patterns (except for Oregon, which had already reapportioned both houses before *Baker v. Carr*, but which redrew congressional boundaries in 1965). It seemed clear that

SCORECARD ON REAPPORTIONMENT

the vast majority of states would hold their 1966 legislative elections on the basis of equal representation for both houses.

Consequences of Unbalanced Representation

ON THE TWO-PARTY SYSTEM. The far-reaching effects of rural legislative advantage are not always sufficiently appreciated. Whenever "rotten borough" situations have aroused publicity the problem is often treated in isolation, as though the controversy concerned only cities versus farmers. Such a view obscures the widespread ramifications of urban-rural representation. One of the most important effects of a distorted legislative pattern concerns the political party balance. In a number of states the party split bears a high correlation to the extent of urbanism. As a general rule, the Democratic party in the industrialized states of the North and Midwest is stronger in city districts, while Republicans usually find most solid support in rural, small-town, and suburban regions. However, in some border states—Oklahoma, Kentucky, and Maryland are examples—Republican support is often weaker in rural than in urban and suburban areas. This is becoming increasingly true also in some parts of the South, where a sizable increase in Republican urban voting strength has long been minimized by the apportionment system. With the major electoral decisions in the South still made in the Democratic party primary, intraparty factionalism typically finds the more liberal Democratic elements stronger in urban areas. In fact, the hard core of Southern conservatism has traditionally been the rural "black belt," where a small white minority, grossly overrepresented in state legislatures as well as in other political institutions of the section, has exercised enormous power.[10]

With this general situation in mind, it is obvious that a representative system allowing urban areas less legislative strength than their populations merit gave an immediate advantage to the political party or faction that is stronger in smaller towns and rural areas. This could result in legislative control by the actual minority party, even in states that vote heavily in the opposite direction. In other instances, even if the successful party represented a popular majority, its legislative strength was often greatly bloated due to a monopoly of rural seats. In New York the two-party struggle is closely contested, and statewide offices might go to either party. But the state legislature was frequently termed "Republican by constitutional law." Since New York City is heavily Democratic and the upstate region largely Republican, the impact of city underrepresentation was apparent. The situation was reversed across the continent in Arizona, where Republicans (heavily concentrated in the two most urban counties) have managed to gain several major statewide offices, but comprised a distinct minority in the legislature, especially the rural-based senate. And in traditionally Democratic Oklahoma, Henry Bellmon became the first Republican governor in the state's history, with a comfortable margin in the 1962 election. But while Republican legislative candidates in Oklahoma also did much better than previously, they were hopelessly outnumbered in both houses (38 to 6 and 95 to 25), due in part to underrepresentation of urban centers.

One consequence of an apportionment system that favors less populous areas in either house is the increased likelihood of divided government. In some cases the party receiving a popular statewide majority controlled one house while the minority had an advantage in the other because it elected more legislators from overrepresented areas. In other states divided control took the form of a governor elected by a statewide majority that was still unable to control one or both houses of the legislature. Table 5 illustrates some past examples of divided government in several states.

The figures in the table reveal sharp disparities in par-

TABLE 5

Years of Party Control in Selected States
1947–1965

State	Senate		House			Governorship	
	D	R	D	R	Tie	D	R
Illinois	0	18	4	14		8	10
New Jersey	0	18	6	12		10	8
Michigan	0	18	0	16	2	14	4
Connecticut	12	6	2	16		12	6
New Mexico	18	0	16	2		10	8
Maryland	18	0	18	0		10	8

SOURCE: Adapted from Malcolm E. Jewell, *The State Legislature: Politics and Practice* (New York: Random House, 1962), p. 11. Data for Maryland have been added to the figures drawn from portions of Jewell's table. Other figures have been updated to include sessions ending in early 1965.

tisan success in each house of the legislature and in seeking the governorship. Since the state executive is chosen at large, his election is generally a more accurate index of popular feeling than the election of a legislature whose electoral districts are distorted for partisan or rural advantage. While many other factors—including weak local party organization, less well-known candidates, and "wasted" votes through heavy concentration of party strength in one or a few areas—can contribute to a discrepancy between a party's statewide and legislative strength, the examples in Table 5 also suggest the importance of disproportionate representation. Illinois and New Jersey are states that had a close two-party struggle for the governorship during the years covered. Democrats were also able to control the more popularly based lower house on some occasions, but the area-based senates were invulnerable bulwarks for the Republicans regardless of statewide voting trends. Michigan Democrats suffered from both "wasted" votes concentrated in urban centers, and underrepresentation of these areas in both houses, but particularly the senate. Connecticut is a two-party state where the vote for governor and the population-based senate tend to coincide. But in the lower house, based on towns, the Republicans held solid majorities with one "freak" exception in the 1958 election, when a 62 percent landslide gave the Democrats a slim majority, their first since 1876. The situation returned to normal in 1960. Finally, New Mexico and Maryland are examples of Democratic advantage through rural-oriented apportionments. Statewide offices were closely contested, but the legislatures were overwhelmingly Democratic.

Even in states where one party is traditionally dominant, disproportionate representation has contributed to weakening the minority party still further, both in numbers elected and in the general discouraging effect on the zeal with which the party contests many constituencies. Florida furnished an excellent example of a growing minority party held severely in check by the legislative apportionment pattern. The state's rapid urbanization has greatly strengthened Republican opposition, with that party's candidate for governor in 1960 taking 40 percent of the statewide vote. But the northern influx of Republican voters to Florida's cities and suburbs had made little dent on the state's heavily rural legislature; in that same 1960 election only seven Republicans won election to the lower house of ninety-five members, a high point which receded to five two years later. During the same period only one senator out of thirty-eight was a Republican. The impact of reapportionment on a minority party's fortunes was clearly demonstrated when Florida, under judicial prodding after *Baker v. Carr*, partially reapportioned its lower house in 1963. In a special election that year, Republicans contested twenty-seven of the twenty-eight new seats in metropolitan areas where the party had been making some effort, winning eleven, thus increasing their total house membership from five to sixteen.

The effect upon the two-party system within the states is surely one of the most telling indictments that can be brought against a condition of representative inequality. The whole rationale of the two-party system is that it should offer the electorate alternative choices of candidates and programs. In this way the parties give meaning and purpose to public sentiment and also serve to strengthen the element of responsibility among governing officials. Ideally, parties should contest for public support in such a way that votes can be translated into some sort of public policy. In a democracy there should be a reasonably direct relationship between predominant public opinion and the power to govern. With this in mind, the implications of a distorted pattern of representation are obvious. How meaningful is an election in which one party is guaranteed, in advance, control of the legislature (or of one of its houses) even if a substantial vote is cast against it? Yet such a result has occurred in several American states frequently enough to raise serious questions for a people that supposedly professes democracy as a value system.

While political parties in many states are not noted for having a high degree of internal cohesion or unity of purpose, there are often issues on which the party balance can make a decided difference. This is particularly true when the governorship is held by a popular leader who has dramatized certain matters of public policy. Yet a misrepresentative legislature (or even one house) can nullify whatever attempt is made to embody into law a program apparently endorsed by the electorate. Even a governor's choice of his own cabinet and other important appointive posts must often meet the approval of a hostile upper house.

To criticize divided government is not to rule out the role of compromise. Differences of opinions and approaches within and between parties and branches of government will inevitably demand conciliation, without the added handicaps of a structural framework that typically fosters irresponsibility or stalemate. After a close analysis of the problem, Malcolm E. Jewell concluded that "compromise in divided state governments is too often simply bargaining for favors, organized bilateral logrolling." And Jewell added perceptively: "The most valid criticism of an apportionment system that encourages divided government is that it breeds irresponsibility. Both parties can make promises that need not be kept because the other party can be blamed for inaction."[11]

ON INTRAPARTY STRUCTURE. In addition to affecting the two-party balance, rural dominance has also played an important role *within* each party. Legislative districts or county units have commonly served as the basis for party organizations, with a consequent advantage for rural leaders. State central committees as well as state conventions of the major parties have usually reflected urban underrepresentation. The make-up of conventions is especially important in those few states where party nominees are selected by the convention method rather than the direct primary.

The apportionment pattern can have other consequences within a party. As we have seen, one of the parties in two-party states frequently had an artificial advantage in one or both houses because its actual electoral strength was magnified in the number of seats held. Yet, paradoxically, this was also a source of weakness. Gubernatorial candidates of the weaker party frequently found their campaigns handicapped by the kind of records established by their party's legislators. Examples are Kentucky and Rhode Island, where statewide Republican candidates had to appeal to the significant urban and suburban vote, but where the party's legislative delegations reflected a largely rural or small-town composition and a more conservative record on political issues.[12]

It is in the one-party states, however, where the party's organization, rules, and practices are of particular importance. In most of the South the Democratic primary is the only effective election. Until 1963 the most noteworthy instance of rural-urban representative imbalance was the Georgia county unit system, under which there was no necessary relationship between the popular vote and the nominations for statewide and congressional offices. Instead, every county was granted twice as many unit votes as it had representatives in the legislature, with each county recorded as a unit for the leading candidate within its boundaries. The long-existing apportionment formula for Georgia's lower house meant that about 22 percent of the state's population, located in the smallest counties, could not only elect a majority of the house, but could also produce a majority of unit votes for the other offices. Georgia's most populous county, Fulton (Atlanta), with a 1960 population of 556,326, had no more strength in either the lower house or in statewide primary elections than the state's three least inhabited counties with a combined population of only 6,980. Under the county unit system, candidates for governor, United States Senator, and other offices could, and sometimes did, win the nomination (and hence the election) without even a plurality of the popular vote. In addition, such an electoral arrangement meant that candidates made little attempt to gain a popular majority, but instead directed their programs and appeals to the small, rural districts with the preponderant political weight.

One of the earliest and most promising consequences of the Supreme Court's 1962 decision in *Baker v. Carr* was the judicial invalidation of Georgia's county unit system, which had survived several previous legal challenges. On the basis of a Federal district court ruling after the Baker decision, the state Democratic Committee decided to hold the 1962 primary election for statewide offices on a popular vote basis. For the first time in half a century, Georgia's urban voters had a proportionate weight in choosing such officials. On March 18, 1963, the United States Supreme Court decided the case on appeal and ruled out the kind of unequal voting inherent in the county unit system as a violation of the Fourteenth Amendment's equal protection clause. While sidestepping any application of its decision to legislative districts, the high tribunal, speaking through Justice Douglas, declared: "Once the geographical unit for which a representative is to be chosen is designated, all who participate in the election are to have an equal vote —whatever their race, whatever their sex, whatever their occupation, whatever their income, and wherever their home may be in that geographical unit." [13] The state of Maryland had long employed a county unit system for primaries similar to Georgia's, but the consequences were less severe, since voters did have a choice between two major parties in the final general election. While the Maryland legislature refused to abandon the system after the judicial decisions in the Georgia case, a three-judge Federal court soon invalidated the Maryland county unit practice on the basis of the precedent established in the Georgia case.

ON SOCIAL AND ECONOMIC POLICIES. While numerous factors, both formal and informal, determine the political product, the structural characteristics of government itself are important elements in the evolution of public policy. Thus a legislative system based upon an unequal allocation of popular strength yields special advantages to certain interest groups and makes the articulation of other groups more difficult. The long-standing over-representation of rural areas meant that organized agricultural interests were usually in a favorable position to influence state legislation. At the same time the system placed certain urban interest groups at a disadvantage. Those urban interests whose policies were compatible with the general outlook of rural representatives were, however, in a more favorable position. In their perceptive analysis of the legislative process in Florida, William Havard and Loren Beth pointed out in 1962 that the heavy rural bias in the apportionment of both houses "obviously gives some pressure groups privileged access to the legislature by providing them with a sure bloc of friendly legislators who hold a majority or close to it." [14]

These authors added that the strongest interest groups in rural Florida included the Farm Bureau and the phosphate and wood-pulp industries. In addition to these were a host of large and small business interests (banks, utilities, insurance companies) that were not particularly rural, but that were powerful in rural areas and thus were in a better position to influence a majority of legislators than were groups confined only to metropolitan areas.

Such facts help explain the behavior of some urban business interests that have staunchly defended inequitable representation for their own areas. These groups apparently found greater representation for their political outlook among rural delegates. The alliance is not surprising in view of the frequent similarity in attitudes held by both interests. In addition, representatives from rural constituencies are often not farmers, but small-town lawyers and businessmen. On many issues they share a natural community of interests with city groups representing a similar social and economic outlook. By contrast, other urban interests, notably labor groups, seldom find support from rural representatives.

An interesting example of certain urban attitudes on representation can be found in California, where the "Federal Plan," restricting each county to only one seat in the state senate, found its main support among such groups as the state Chamber of Commerce and most of the urban press. Opponents of the system periodically sought its modification, primarily through initiative campaigns in 1948, 1960, and 1962. While the less populous counties naturally opposed any change, the major battles took place within the large metropolitan counties that would have multiplied their legislative strength. Not until the 1962 campaign did a proposal attract the support of significant interests and the daily press in Los Angeles, while the northern urban bay area consistently fought any plan from which Los Angeles County would be the largest beneficiary. The 1962 initiative, which lost in a fairly close vote, was the most moderate of the ballot measures yet attempted. It would have retained the existing forty-district pattern, but would have added ten seats for the most populous counties. The list of major financial contributors to the campaign against the proposition hardly looks like a constellation of agrarian forces: the Pacific Gas and Electric Company, the Standard Oil Company of California, the Southern Pacific Railroad, the Richfield Oil Company, the Bank of America, plus several other oil companies, banks, and railroads.[15]

Recognition of a heterogeneous framework of interests is helpful in understanding the difficulty long encountered by labor and consumer groups in influencing state legislative decisions on social and economic policy. A survey of restrictive labor legislation in a number of states revealed the leading role of rural lawmakers, often working with business approval or assistance.[16] Other issues that have characterized distinct urban and rural (or small-town) conflicts include: regulation of wages and hours, protection of migrant workers, distribution of certain tax revenues (especially from gasoline), daylight-saving time, and state aid to roads and education.

It is difficult to pinpoint to what extent the representative pattern of state legislatures has affected the resolution of such issues. For one thing, influences on the legislative product are myriad, and variables differ in relative importance from state to state. It appears that the apportionment structure has been highly significant in affecting policy outcomes in some states, while in others it has had only a slight or negligible bearing, at least on *positive* enactments of public policy.[17] To predict how a differently constituted legislature *would* act was even more difficult until the recent revolution in legislative patterns stimulated by judicial pressure. Now, comparative studies of policy questions within a state before and after a comprehensive reapportionment should be most informative. Judging from the amount of concern, money, time, and effort expended by differing interest groups in so many states over proposed reapportionments, it is clear that major segments of society and economic interests have at least assumed that the make-up of the legislature makes a difference in the real world of policy formation. In many cases the impact of legislative representation seems pervasive but not always easily measurable. As Professors Havard and Beth concluded in their detailed study of legislative politics in Florida: "The fact that no simple cause and effect sequence can be ascribed to the influence of the apportionment system does not bear out the claim that the system has no substantive effect on public affairs; instead it indicates that the influences are in most cases subtle and deeply embedded in the structure of government." [18]

As this discussion of public policy has already indicated, inaction can be as important as positive legislative action. Some interest groups gain their objectives mainly through affirmative enactments, whereas others rely primarily on inaction and delay. The traditional American institutions of separation of powers and checks and balances, specifically devised to discourage positive government, give an immediate advantage to those groups benefiting mostly from inaction. In state legislatures a further check was frequently established by a pattern of representation that placed additional obstacles in the path of interests that otherwise might have influenced more directly the formulation of public policy.

State Government: Past and Future

For years many states have had legislatures heavily influenced by rural and small-town minorities, but governors more responsive to the entire state, including metropolitan interests. While the system of separation of governmental functions inevitably invites legislative-executive friction, this has often been further aggravated when each branch was accountable to different publics. Resulting stalemates tended to give a negative cast to public policy, with an accompanying diffusion of responsibility. A good example is the state of Michigan, where a Democratic governor and a Republican legislature were chronically deadlocked over state tax and fiscal policies through most of the 1950's.

The recruitment of political leadership has also been influenced by inflated rural power. In many states opportunities for advancement within both legislature and political parties have been greater for small-town politicians. This has been especially noticeable in the South, though it was likely to be found elsewhere to a greater extent than is generally realized.

The failure of state governments to adapt themselves to contemporary needs has been a subject of increasing concern. While there are numerous reasons for the archaic institutions that have characterized many states, the possibility of change or reform has long been blocked by rural-urban or sectional antagonisms. Movements for much-needed constitutional conventions inevitably encountered roadblocks due to widespread fears of more representative legislatures. This has probably been the greatest single cause of resistance to basic constitutional change. Successful movements in the rewriting of state constitutions were usually possible only when urban areas accepted a perpetuation of their subordinate role.

Moreover, the growing habit of some sections of the public to try to enact policy directly, by-passing the legislatures entirely, was sometimes ascribed to dissatisfaction with malapportionment. The participants in the Eighth American Assembly in 1955 commented:

> The majority often looks solely to the governor who has been elected on a statewide basis; it adopts constitutional amendments that are in effect statutory measures; it writes into the constitution detailed restrictions on the scope of the

legislature's powers; it displaces the legislature through excessive use of the initiative and referendum; or, it turns too often to the national Congress for relief. These are some of the results of a bad apportionment system.[19]

Finally, a less tangible matter that appears to be a partial consequence of the problem of representation is the question of public confidence in state governments. Closely related is the ability of these governmental units to adapt themselves to the needs of contemporary society. A legislature that is able to stymie the enactment of popularly endorsed programs is hardly in a position to inspire public confidence. While representative equality is hardly a panacea for the many problems facing state government now and in the future, its realization should at least clarify the question of responsibility and perhaps provide a sounder psychological climate for political institutions.

CHAPTER 4

Metropolitan America: New Dimension of Rural-Urban Conflict

Those who labor in the earth are the chosen people of God, if ever He had a chosen people, whose breasts He has made His peculiar deposit for substantial and genuine virtue. . . . The mobs of great cities add just so much to the support of pure government, as sores do to the strength of the human body.

THOMAS JEFFERSON

This sentiment, expressed by early America's greatest democrat, is of more than historical interest. It has symbolized an enduring part of this nation's heritage. The virtues of agrarian life have always had an enormous appeal to the average American. Even many city dwellers, themselves usually no more than a generation or two removed from the farm, tend to look upon urban life with suspicion.

Though the United States has become predominantly urban during the twentieth century, the image of rural virtues and the superiority of rural life persists. This shift over the past generation from a rural to an urban society has taken place so rapidly—almost suddenly—that attitudes have understandably lagged. Thus the traditional American ideal of the virtuous, self-reliant farmer with his roots in the soil has cast an uncritical bias on a considerable amount of public opinion. The city has been regarded as the source of corruption and immorality, while the countryside supposedly preserves the virtues of honesty, thrift, and character. Farmers, we are often reminded, constitute the very "backbone of democracy."

How realistic are such stereotypes? The indictment against city life generally stresses political corruption and notorious bossism; implicit also is a distasteful view of some adverse effects of industrialization upon cities: congestion, slums, and crime—conditions inevitably contrasted with the imagined bucolic splendor and innocence of agrarian life. This picture, however, is one-sided. While cities are open to some blame on all of these scores, they can proudly boast of some uniquely urban contributions to society, notably the fostering of cultural activities and of intellectual and social freedom. And many ignore the fact that slums are by no means confined to cities. Decaying rural areas are often deficient in both material and cultural advantages. A. Whitney Griswold, the late President of Yale University, once observed: "A self-sufficient farm in our time is more likely to be a haunt of illiteracy and malnutrition than a wellspring of democracy." [1]

On the political side of rural-urban differences are two additional factors worth stressing. One is that civic reform movements and governmental reorganization have made enormously greater strides in cities over the past half century than on either the county or state level. Second, political machines and bosses are by no means confined to urban areas. Rural machines are less colorful and dramatic and far less publicized, but their existence and power cannot be ignored. A lifelong student of rural government attested that "It is safe to say that in nine-tenths of the counties in the United States public affairs are in the hands of what the irreverent call the 'court-house gang.' . . . The doings of the gang are perhaps not so dramatic as the gorgeous pillagings of a Tweed . . . and they have certainly not had as good a press, but no veteran need feel diffident in the presence of his urban brethren." [2]

However unjustified it may be, the traditional American distrust of the city unquestionably underlies and explains many of the limitations on urban legislative representation outlined in Chapter 3. A defender of California's rural-based senate expressed a sentiment that is probably paralleled in many other states when he said:

> While the attitude of the average Californian toward the government of the State's most populous centers is one of confidence, that confidence does not signify the willingness to surrender to these metropolitan areas the power to control both houses of the Legislature. With all the pride he has in the traditions and the phenomenal development of these great cities, he remembers that they are great cities, and subject to the same political phenomena which characterize all congested centers of population.[3]

Population Growth and Trends

Whatever stereotypes have prevailed concerning urban life and political power, the complexity of population growth had by the 1960's rendered much of the terminology dated, if not meaningless. Between 1910 and 1930 the United States shifted from a rural to an urban nation, until by 1960 the Bureau of the Census classified 69.9 percent of the total population as urban. And by far the greatest part of the urban residents had congregated in metropolitan areas (containing a core city of 50,000 or more, plus a suburban fringe). Moreover, the period since World War II has witnessed the swift rise of suburbia, adding a new dimension to the old rural-urban dichotomy. In the decade preceding 1960, no less than two thirds of the nation's entire population increase took the form of suburban growth.[4] At the same time, the numerical strength of core cities had neared the saturation point, with the population of most of the largest municipalities actually declining. Urban problems characteristically took new forms, as the metropolitan proliferation spilled over a variety of city, county, special district, and even state boundaries. In the perceptive words of Victor Jones, "The people of the United States have become metropolitan before realizing their change from a rural to an urban nation."[5]

The old stereotype of a single "urban" interest is even more invalid in view of the complexity of economic and political forces ushered in by metropolitanism. The problems facing cities tend to be considerably different in nature and scope from those that concern the suburbs. To be sure, it is difficult to generalize even within these categories; but a fairly common pattern can be found in much of metropolitan America. For one thing, as Professor Jones observed, "The central city has become the haven, or perhaps more accurately, the loosely defined ghetto of those who are not wealthy enough, or through restrictive measures are not allowed, to settle in the suburbs."[6] Minority groups, particularly Negroes, have tended increasingly to congregate in the core cities, as many middle-class whites move out to the suburbs. The Chicago area, where Negroes comprise approximately 23 percent of the city's population but less than 3 percent in the suburbs, is fairly typical of the nation's two dozen largest cities.[7]

Aside from social and racial differences, several political and economic issues tend to distinguish central cities from suburbs. The latter, being newer and largely residential communities, experience the problems of rapid growth and need for a variety of services. Socially more homogeneous than the city, suburbia tends to display a nonpartisan, "good government" emphasis on local matters, frequently with a preponderantly one-party identity for state and national politics. In contrast, the city is more preoccupied with physical decay, congestion, public safety, traffic, and housing. "The character of these kinds of problems along with the very heterogeneity of the large city," David Minar and Scott Greer conclude, "are more likely to require a politics of bargaining and accommodation, less likely to permit a politics in which issues are hidden under expertness or satisfactorily handled through technical treatment." [8] Frequently accompanying these general divergences in political issues are differences in attitude, with many suburbanites "anti-city" in outlook.[9] Any city-suburban frictions, however subtle, are likely to hamper efforts to resolve some of the metropolitan problems affecting the entire area.

Legislative Representation of Cities and Suburbs

In view of the marked disparities in the growth rates of cities and suburbs, it is clear that the representative status of both urban and suburban communities will usually have changed. If a city's population has declined in relation to that of the whole state, then its representative status has improved—unless it has been changed by redistricting. On the other hand, a fast-growing suburb may progressively lose ground in relative representative strength. The study on representative inequality by Professors David and Eisenberg (referred to in the previous chapter) threw some light on the differential status of several urban and suburban localities in the nation's largest metropolitan areas. Table 6 includes a selected sample of their findings. As in the earlier tables, values under 100 indicate underrepresentation and those over 100, overrepresentation. Counties were used as the standard of measurement that could be applied in all fifty states. For this reason, the urban-suburban distinction is not precise, since a city's fringe growth within its own

TABLE 6

Relative Value of Representative Strength in State Legislatures for Selected Metropolitan Areas

Central City and Suburban Counties	1910	1930	1950	1960
New York City	75	71	81	93
Nassau County	122	54	101	59
Rockland County	132	127	108	86
Suffolk County	113	79	100	47
Westchester County	117	88	109	95
Philadelphia City	89	88	88	98
Bucks County	148	147	124	83
Chester County	121	131	113	92
Delaware County	112	67	67	55
Montgomery County	89	80	72	53
Suffolk County (Boston)	104	91	99	123
Essex County	102	106	110	110
Middlesex County	100	101	98	92
Norfolk County	99	119	100	83
Plymouth County	109	115	108	91
St. Louis City	69	67	74	92
Jefferson County	90	99	79	62
St. Charles County	93	105	96	71
St. Louis County	67	38	71	45
Baltimore City	44	51	62	83
Anne Arundel County	125	125	83	62
Baltimore County	51	55	36	26
Hennepin County (Minneapolis)	85	67	60	55
Ramsey County (St. Paul)	84	80	76	73
Anoka County	93	95	71	39
Dakota County	93	84	68	49
Washington County	120	156	130	98
Fulton County (Atlanta)	24	15	12	12
Clayton County	77	77	125	82
Cobb County	95	84	75	49
DeKalb County	95	61	37	23
Gwinnett County	104	125	70	56
Denver City	72	69	78	87
Adams County	109	74	98	44
Arapahoe County	79	70	73	46
Boulder County	78	95	81	70
Jefferson County	123	95	71	41

SOURCE: David and Eisenberg, *op. cit.*, pp. 12–13.

county is part of that county's population and is classed with its central city. Only the suburban growth in adjoining counties is reflected.

As this table indicates, many cities actually improved their representation relative to population over the years, though they still usually lagged behind their proportionate share. But suburban growth caused adjoining counties to suffer a devalued weight that is usually progressive and sometimes dramatic in extent. Among the thirteen largest metropolitan areas (in population) the central cities improved their positions in all but two instances (where the values remained constant). But the relative position of the central-city county improved in only four of the remaining fourteen metropolitan areas studied by David and Eisenberg, while in the others it usually declined slightly or remained stable. The main reason for this difference is found in the use of county units as the data for measurement. In the most populous (usually eastern) metropolitan areas the core cities tend to occupy their entire counties (which are also often geographically smaller). Yet in the less populous metropolitan areas there is usually more room for expansion of the city and its suburbs within its own county.[10]

The population trends indicated in Table 6 clearly suggest that future legislative reapportionments resulting from judicial prodding will primarily benefit suburban areas, though many cities would probably also make moderate to substantial gains.

Consequences for Urban Areas

The underrepresentation of metropolitan areas in state legislatures entails definite and important consequences for urban governmental units. While every municipality faces certain unique problems, there are numerous fields of more or less common concern to city officials. Much state legislation, including vital taxation and grant-in-aid policies, bears a direct relationship to local units. The amount of flexibility allowed localities in handling their own affairs is often a source of contention as well. A sympathetic and cooperative attitude by the state is usually essential if municipalities are to give adequate attention to the increasingly complex problems of an urban and industrial society.

In actual practice, of course, cities are often handicapped by restrictive state policies. Antagonism between the states and their growing urban centers became especially acute since the balance of population shifted to the cities while the balance of political power remained in the rural and small town regions. For several years the United States Conference of Mayors, composed of the elected leaders of the nation's urban governments, singled out unequal representation as the major source of trouble for municipalities in general. The organization has asserted that most urban residents were virtual "second class citizens" and were the victims of "taxation without representation." Mayors and city managers in all parts of the nation have objected to the inferior status allowed municipalities in state lawmaking bodies. While at least part of this protest can doubtless be ascribed to the tendency of officials at any level to blame higher units of government for their troubles, nevertheless a good deal of the urban case seems well documented. City spokesmen have pointed specifically to discriminatory practices regarding taxation policies, state services and grants-in-aid, and state interference with local freedom of action.[11]

Substantial disparities in the distribution of state tax funds frequently seemed directly traceable to the legislative underrepresentation of urban communities. An extreme instance could be found in Florida, where the rural counties heavily dominated both houses of the legislature. Some of that state's taxes, including lucrative race-track revenues, were distributed equally among Florida's sixty-seven counties. Hugh Douglas Price reported (in 1962) the following situation:

For some of the smaller counties, the state largess is so great that local taxes are almost unnecessary. Thus the amount of racing revenue returned amounts to only 20 cents per person per year for Dade County, but runs as high as $61.07 per person in one of the smallest counties. The race-track fund alone can account for the bigger part of a small county's general and school funds. For counties of under 10,000, the racing fund accounts, on the average, for 42.99 per cent of county school funds (the high was 87.26 per cent) and for 30.36 per cent of county general funds (the high was 64.76 per cent). This almost incredible form of allocation was satisfactory to the racing interests, since it provided a politically impregnable basis for legal race-track betting.[12]

An almost classic example of city-state friction has been the relationship of New York City to the state house in Albany. It must be stressed that sectional conflict in New York State cannot accurately be described as urban versus rural. Upstate areas contain a number of large municipalities, but most of them are usually politically allied with rural areas against the metropolitan center.

Fear and jealousy of the big city by the rest of the state long resulted in an inferior status for New York City in both houses of the legislature. Generations ago, shrewd and farsighted upstate politicians, aware of the city's potential growth, made sure that it would never elect a majority of the legislature, regardless of its population. The state constitution of 1894 placed virtually permanent control of both houses in the upstate region.

One of the most noticeable effects of metropolitan underrepresentation in New York was on the major party balance. Since the city is strongly Democratic and the rest of the state (except for certain pockets of Democratic strength) is heavily Republican, it took a landslide of almost miraculous proportions to remove the GOP from control of the legislature. In modern times this has happened only twice—in 1934 and 1964. Republican-directed redistrictings after each census double-locked the advantage to the GOP already frozen into the state constitution. Between 1938 and 1965 the Republicans controlled both houses with at least 55 percent of the seats, even in years of Democratic statewide success. When New York was under court order to reapportion both houses on a population basis, Governor Rockefeller called a special session for December of 1964 so that the task could be accomplished before the Democrats, as a result of the November landslide, would take control during the regular 1965 session.

In view of this background, political tensions in New York between the state government and the large metropolis are understandable. The fact that the party split also reflects the sectional antagonism tends to re-emphasize the divergent points of view. Moreover, judicial interpretations of the state constitution do not allow the city a generous degree of home rule, thus authorizing the legislature to pass judgment on a variety of city actions. For example, the city can claim for its own needs only those taxing powers permitted it by the state. The state's insistence that grants of taxing power to the city be short-term has further aggravated the relationship. As a result, city officials must make annual trips to Albany (with "hat in hand," according to them) before they can determine revenue sources for a city budget that typically exceeds the amount of the entire state budget. Leaders of New York City have also protested its share of state-aid revenues in comparison with those allotted to other localities. All of these fiscal issues become the battleground for bitter debate and widespread publicity during every session of the legislature and during election campaigns.[13] One example of the perpetual controversy is furnished by Edward C. Banfield and James Q. Wilson:

In 1959, the New York City Council adopted by a vote of 23 to 1 a resolution that a committee be appointed to study the possibility and legality of the city's seceding from New York State and constituting itself an independent, fifty-first state. If this half-serious proposal had been adopted, the city could have kept over two billion dollars a year in taxes which now go to Albany.[14]

Since the state would have to agree to a secession, this was a futile gesture by the city's legislators.

We must be careful, however, not to overgeneralize about the role of legislative apportionment in affecting urban governments. It is commonly an important consideration, but its impact varies from state to state, depending upon the strength of other variables, such as the party system, partisan geography, home rule, traditions, state leadership, local leadership, and socio-economic patterns. A proportionate share of legislative representation for a city is not necessarily any guarantee of favorable treatment by the state. As an example, Banfield and Wilson cite Boston, where "State Senator John Powers has as much to say about its affairs as does Mayor John Collins." [15] Moreover, since cities typically manifest internal divisions on some questions of local (as well as state) policy, a city's legislative delegation may reflect this split and weaken the positions of mayors and councils. Finally, the growth of suburbia frequently projects into the legislative arena some of the political divergences within the larger metropolitan area.[16]

A final consequence which many observers attributed to unrepresentative state legislatures was the extent of direct relationships between cities and agencies of the Federal government. Especially over the past thirty years, Federal-municipal ties have developed in a number of important fields. In 1955 the Commission on Intergovernmental Relations, appointed by President Eisenhower, noted that legislative neglect of urban communities had increasingly led many people to look to Washington for more services. "One result of State neglect of the reapportionment problem," suggested the Commission, "is that urban governments have bypassed the States and made direct cooperative arrangements with the National Government in such fields as housing and urban development, airports, and defense community facilities."[17] While admitting the necessity of some of these relationships, the Commission added that they have tended to weaken the state's control and authority.

• • •

As this chapter has indicated, the whole question of urban representation has been complicated by a number of forces, notably population mobility in general and the mushrooming growth of suburbia in particular. Nor have rural regions escaped these trends. Many counties that only recently were rural or small-town in make-up have become the home of proliferating suburbs. Industry as well as population has begun to decentralize, leaving central cities and locating in areas that were formerly countryside. Politically speaking, the entire question of urban versus rural groupings must be viewed in new perspective. The matter has been suggestively put by Robert S. Friedman:

> Stated differently, conflicts which superficially may be described as setting urban areas against rural areas are more satisfactorily explained in terms of conflict among social, economic, and cultural interests which have incidentally been associated with urban and rural areas, at least in the past. Present trends, in the United States, find these interests rearranging themselves in such a way that within the foreseeable future the ability to describe conflict in terms of urban-rural difference, even superficially, will disappear.[18]

This does not, of course, mean that an end is in sight to political conflicts that appear to be rural versus urban or big city versus upstate or downstate. What it does mean is that such simple terminology increasingly obscures the actual interests—economic, social, or partisan

—involved in the struggle. Nor will legislative representation cease to be a crucial element, even if geographic aggregates do not neatly delineate the identification of major interests.

Finally, fast-moving and complex population trends may engender some interesting shifts in attitudes. Communities that once identified themselves with the agrarian status quo have found that the representative shoe pinched and sought a greater voice in the legislature. At the same time, declining districts in some cities (and even a few cities as a whole) displayed the resistance to change that was formerly characteristic only of rural forces (and their allies elsewhere). Indeed, this prospect in itself reveals the inherent strength of the representative principle: one man, one vote. For its embodiment in an electoral system can most readily reflect complex social changes in an institutional form that is not tied to one era of population distribution only. A similar point was well expressed in these words of the Commission on Intergovernmental Relations:

> Reapportionment should not be thought of solely in terms of a conflict of interests between urban and rural areas. In the long run, the interests of all in an equitable system of representation that will strengthen State government is far more important than any temporary advantage to an area enjoying overrepresentation.[19]

CHAPTER 5

Representation at the National Level

The common association of unequal political power with state governments has often obscured its importance at the national level. Yet the patterns that have so long characterized most state legislatures had their impact on Congress as well. In this and other ways, the question of representation has played a significant—though frequently less obvious—role in the nation's policy-making institutions.

The United States Senate and Urbanism

Until recently it had been traditional to consider the equal representation of states in the United States Senate as the chief national manifestation of overrepresented rural power.[1] Indeed, the distortions from the ideal of "one man, one vote" are greater in the national upper house than was ever the case with most state legislatures. The constitutional compromise of 1787, arrived at when the union was a far looser federation than it later became, has vested tremendous power in thinly populated areas. Today the ten most populous states contain over half of the nation's inhabitants, but have only twenty Senators, while the remaining states elect eighty. Moreover, a Senate majority made up of the twenty-six least populous states would represent only about 17 percent of the nation's population. While this is a "theoretical control" percentage, certain "real life" issues occasionally entail a basic sectional split, with a corresponding disparity between population and Senate strength. An interesting example was the battle in 1959 over filibuster reform. A bipartisan proposal to allow a simple majority of the entire Senate to invoke cloture after fifteen days of debate went down to a crushing defeat by a vote of 67 to 28. Yet this large Senate majority (with its core of strength in the Solid South and sparsely populated Great Plains and Rocky Mountain regions) actually represented a minority of the nation's voters.

Another result of this disproportionate representation in the American federal system has been the advantage held by economic interests located in the less populous states. Historically these interests have been mainly agricultural or mining. The most striking example is an entire region of thinly populated states, the Rocky Mountain area. The disproportionate influence of Senators from that region has frequently been noticeable in legislation affecting economic activities common to much of the region. Silver mining and sugar beet interests have often received preferential national attention. If one takes into consideration only the effective voting population, the South is another region that historically has been overrepresented in the Senate, and Southern interests have often benefited. It is a rare piece of protective farm legislation that does not include cotton, peanuts, rice, and tobacco among the most "basic" crops.

Despite the disparity in the size of Senate constituencies, the traditional view that the result is *rural* overrepresentation has to be modified for two reasons. One is that the degree of urbanism has become sufficiently widespread so that the number of preponderantly rural states is rapidly declining. According to the classification of the 1960 census, thirty-nine of the fifty states are more urban than rural, with twenty-nine of these claiming 60 percent or more of their population as urban. The second reason is the fact that a state's two Senators are elected at large and must appeal to as many significant interests within the state as possible. Even many rural states have a substantial urban populace that cannot be ignored. Thus most Senators can be expected to be actively aware of urban interests and problems.

The Lower House: How Representative?

Ironically, a good case could be made for the proposition that the Senate, with broader-based constituencies, has for some period of time been more representative in respect to urban and rural political power than the lower house of Congress, supposedly based on a general population standard. Due partly to the impact of unrepresentative state legislatures on the make-up of congressional districts, the House of Representatives long reflected marked deviations from a standard of equality. The fact that the disparities became generally greater with the passage of time may suggest one reason for the intervention of the United States Supreme Court early in 1964 in its landmark decision on congressional districting. While *Wesberry v. Sanders* affected only the state of Georgia (and resulted in a prompt redistricting by its legislature), it appears inevitable that the judicial ruling will, within a few years, affect all states with substantial inequalities among congressional constituencies. Because of the contemporary importance of this question, the following analysis is designed to furnish background and perspective for the new direction charted by the Court.

APPORTIONMENT OF CONGRESSIONAL DISTRICTS. Since the Senate represents political units rather than people, it is all the more essential that the lower house of Congress be faithfully designed to reflect population. Indeed, nearly all members of the constitutional convention of 1787 which accepted a compromise Senate were agreed that the House of Representatives must be the "grand depository of the democratic principle." [2] As a result the Constitution stipulated that representatives "shall be apportioned among the several States . . . according to their respective Numbers . . ." (with a minimum of one for each state). The manner of electing the various representatives within each state is left to the respective legislatures, subject to ultimate congressional control. One reason for empowering Congress to alter state regulations or to make new ones is of more than historic interest. James Madison voiced apprehensions that "the inequality of the representation in the legislatures of particular states would produce a like inequality in their representation in the national legislature, as it was presumable that the counties having the power in the former case would secure it to themselves in the latter." [3]

Decennial apportionment statutes passed by Congress over the latter part of the nineteenth century attempted to set standards for states to follow that would assure fair districting. Eventually states were supposed to create congressional districts of compact and contiguous territory, containing "as nearly as practicable" equal numbers of inhabitants. In 1929 Congress adopted an "automatic" reapportionment statute that empowers the President, in the absence of new legislation, to allot the proper number of congressional seats among the states after each census, based on a mathematical formula. However, the former guidelines for fair districting *within* states were omitted, probably because they had not been enforced when in existence.

Since the 1929 act there have been many proposals for new and more precise districting requirements. When President Truman in 1951 announced the new apportionment of representatives as a result of population changes reflected in the 1950 census, he asked Congress to reinstate the former statutory requirement of equal single-member districts, and to require in addition a maximum percentage deviation allowable within any state. Both the President and the reapportionment committee of the American Political Science Association suggested that a maximum deviation of 15 percent both above and below a state's average district population would allow sufficient flexibility. Periodically since that time bills have been introduced in Congress stipulating similar standards, sometimes differing as to the specific percentage range of deviation allowed. Congress showed little enthusiasm for such reform until the Supreme Court's decision in *Wesberry v. Sanders.* In March, 1965, the House of Representatives passed a bill requiring congressional districts to be compact and contiguous and to fall within a population range of 15 percent above and below a state's average. The legislation further prohibited at-large elections for any state with more than one house seat, and restricted states to one valid districting between decennial censuses. The impetus for this set of guidelines was apparently the general desire on the part of Congressmen for protection against even more rigid criteria which they feared the courts might impose if they failed to work out their own standards for districts as allowed Congress under Article I, Section 4 of the Constitution.[4]

In the absence of federal statutory regulation, state legislatures were free to do about as they pleased on the matter of redistricting congressional seats. The implications of this power, combined with the unrepresentative nature of most state legislatures, led to hardly surprising results. State lawmakers were almost as cavalier about periodic equalization of congressional districts as they were about reapportioning their own seats. The only sanction of any consequence that forced some states to act was a change in their total share of House membership. When a state lost congressional strength it had been required either to redistrict or to elect all representatives at large. Since the latter eventuality was usually feared by politicians of both parties, some type of redistricting ordinarily resulted. If a state gained membership, only the additional seat or seats were elected at large in the event of legislative failure to act. This alternative was often chosen when disagreement over districting arose.

INEQUALITIES AMONG CONGRESSIONAL DISTRICTS. The decade from 1950 to 1960 witnessed not only a substantial population increase for the nation as a whole, but enormous shifts of population within and among states. As a result, exactly half of the fifty states were directly affected in the size of their congressional delegations. Of these, sixteen lost from one to three Congressmen, while the other nine gained from one to eight seats. Consequently, these twenty-five were the states that had some impetus to rearrange their constituencies for the lower house of Congress. Nineteen responded by creating new districts, while the remaining six decided upon at-large elections for either one additional Congressman, or for all seats. While the resulting districts in some of the states displayed numerous inequalities, the post-1960 redistricting showed less extreme disparities than was true following the 1950 census.[5] Table 7 lists all the states that created new districts in the period 1961–1962, with the greatest population disparities indicating the most extreme distortions. A brief descriptive reference to the nature of the district or its major city is included in parentheses.

Six of the twenty states included in Table 7—Iowa, Maine, Massachusetts, Minnesota, Nebraska, and North Dakota—were able to keep all district disparities within the frequently proposed range of 15 percent above or below their state averages, while three more—Missouri, New York, and West Virginia—came close. (The national district average would be 410,481, though this necessarily varies for each state.) Also included in the table is the only state that neither gained nor lost a seat

TABLE 7

Congressional Redistricting, 1961–1962

Districts	*Population*	*Districts*	*Population*
ARIZONA		MINNESOTA	
1 (Phoenix)	663,510	5 (Minneapolis)	482,872
3 (rural)	198,236	2 (rural)	375,475
ARKANSAS		MISSISSIPPI	
4 (small town)	575,385	2 (rural)	608,441
2 (Little Rock)	517,860	4 (rural)	295,072
3 (rural)	332,844	MISSOURI	
CALIFORNIA		2 (suburban St. Louis)	505,854
28 (Los Angeles)	588,933	10 (rural)	381,602
5 (San Francisco)	301,172	NEBRASKA	
FLORIDA		1 (small town)	530,507
6 (Ft. Lauderdale and suburbia)	660,345	2 (Omaha)	404,695
9 (small town)	237,235	NEW JERSEY	
ILLINOIS		1 (Camden)	585,586
10 (suburban Chicago)	552,582	14 (Jersey City, Hoboken)	255,165
6 (Chicago City)	278,703	NEW YORK	
IOWA		12 (New York City)	469,908
2 (Dubuque)	442,406	24 (New York City)	348,940
7 (small town)	353,156	NORTH CAROLINA	
KANSAS		8 (Charlotte)	491,461
1 (small town)	539,592	1 (rural)	277,861
5 (small town)	373,583	NORTH DAKOTA	
KENTUCKY		1 (small town)	333,290
3 (Louisville)	610,947	2 (rural)	299,156
1 (rural)	350,839	PENNSYLVANIA	
MAINE		7 (Philadelphia suburbs)	553,154
2 (small town)	505,465	15 (small town)	303,026
1 (mid-urban)	463,800	WEST VIRGINIA	
MASSACHUSETTS		4 (small town)	422,046
9 (Boston)	478,962	5 (rural)	303,098
1 (mid-urban)	376,336		

SOURCE: Population figures and other data obtained from the invaluable publications of the Congressional Quarterly Service, particularly the *Congressional Quarterly Special Report* ("Congressional Redistricting: Impact of the 1960 Census Reapportionment of House Seats"), Sept. 28, 1962. The categories "rural," "small town," "mid-urban," and "metropolitan," are taken from *Congressional Quarterly Weekly Report,* XIV (March 30, 1956), 360. These criteria have been applied to the post-1960 situation in preference to *Congressional Quarterly*'s newer three-classification scheme of urban, suburban, and rural (see *Weekly Report,* February 2, 1962, pp. 153–157) which the author regards as less appropriate than the earlier one, and frequently misleading. For my own tables in this chapter the metropolitan and certain mid-urban districts are more specifically delineated by reference to major cities or suburbs. (For still another classification of districts—this time into four categories of urban, suburban, rural, and mixed—see *Congressional Quarterly Weekly Report* [September 20, 1963], pp. 1642–1657.)

but still redistricted: North Dakota created districts for its two Congressmen in place of its former practice of electing them both at large. While nearly half of the states in the table created equitable districts, the list also shows some substantial disparities. Ratios of 2 to 1 and higher are frequent. The prize for the most ironic inequality shown in Table 7 could well go to Arizona, one of the states with the fastest rate of growth between 1950 and 1960. While the state had only two Congressmen, both districts were equally represented, though by 1960 each was heavily overpopulated in terms of strength in Congress:

Former Districts	*1950 Population*	*1960 Population*	*Percent Increase (Approximate)*
District 1 (Maricopa County)	331,770	663,510	100
District 2 (rest of state)	417,817	638,651	53

The post-1960-census reapportionment allocated a third congressional seat to Arizona. Applying a statute passed back in 1947 in anticipation of an eventual third Representative in Congress, Arizona simply split its less populous Second District into two new constituencies. Yet the fast-growing Phoenix metropolitan area (Maricopa County), the growth of which was most responsible for gaining Arizona a third seat, was "rewarded" by having its congressional representation reduced from one half to one third of the state delegation.

In spite of such inequalities, states that *did* redistrict after the 1960 census came much closer to balanced constituencies than those which took no redistricting action whatever to take account of population shifts. Inaction characterized two different types of states: those that gained or lost congressional strength but could not agree on new districts, and those where there was no such pressure to redistrict. Some states have experienced no

TABLE 8

Outdated Districting, 1963
(No Change in Delegation Size)

Districts	*Population*	*Districts*	*Population*
COLORADO (1912)		OREGON (1941)	
2 (small town) *	653,954	3 (Portland)	522,813
1 (Denver)	493,887	1 (small town) †	517,555
4 (rural)	195,551	1 (rural)	265,164
CONNECTICUT (1931)		SO. CAROLINA (1931)	
1 (Hartford)	589,555	2 (small town)	531,555
4 (Bridgeport)	653,589	5 (rural)	272,220
5 (mid-urban)	318,952	TENNESSEE (1941)	
(1 congressman at large)		9 (Memphis)	627,019
GEORGIA (1931)		8 (rural)	223,387
5 (Atlanta)	823,680	VIRGINIA (1951)	
9 (rural)	272,154	10 (Washington, D.C. suburbs)	539,618
INDIANA (1941)		4 (rural)	312,890
11 (Indianapolis)	697,567	WASHINGTON (1957)	
1 (Gary, E. Chicago)	513,269	7 (South Seattle and suburbs)	510,512
9 (rural)	290,596	3 (small town)	342,540
LOUISIANA (1912)		WISCONSIN (1931) ‡	
6 (Baton Rouge)	536,029	2 (Madison)	530,316
8 (small town)	263,850	5 (No. Milwaukee)	520,674
OKLAHOMA (1951)		4 (So. Milwaukee)	515,367
5 (Oklahoma City)	552,863	10 (rural)	236,870
1 (Tulsa)	521,542		
3 (rural)	227,692		

States with Only Two Representatives

Districts	*Population*	*Districts*	*Population*
IDAHO (1911)		NEW HAMPSHIRE (1881)	
1 (rural)	257,242	1 (mid-urban)	331,818
2 (small town)	409,949	2 (small town)	275,103
MONTANA (1917)		RHODE ISLAND (1931)	
1 (small town)	274,194	1 (metropolitan)	399,782
2 (small town)	400,573	2 (metropolitan)	459,706
SOUTH DAKOTA (1931)		UTAH (1931)	
1 (small town)	497,669	1 (mid-urban)	317,973
2 (small town)	182,845	2 (Salt Lake City)	572,654

* Includes all of suburban Denver.
† Includes much of suburban Portland.
‡ For Wisconsin's redistricting of 1963 see Table 11 and text.
SOURCE: See Table 7.

change in the size of their congressional delegations for as much as half a century. When there was no stimulus for a state to give serious consideration to redistricting, "silent gerrymanders" predictably resulted. Table 8 lists the extreme distortions found in these states as of 1963, with major cities or district characteristics again noted. Date of prior redistricting is also included in parentheses. A separate listing includes states with only two Congressmen, since the extremes in these cases were the only ones present. The inequities are fewer here than in the upper part of the table, largely because these six states are, with the exception of Utah, areas of high population stability. Their delegations have remained at two Representatives for at least three decades. New Hampshire's districts are over eighty years old and still within an equitable population range.

Finally, the greatest of all extremes (as of 1963) in the populations of congressional districts were found in a handful of states that either gained or lost Representatives after the 1960 census, but resorted to the use of at-large elections instead of drawing new district lines. Four of the five states in Table 9 each gained a single Congressman and chose to elect him at-large and let existing districts remain undisturbed. It is not surprising that the greatest population distortions should appear where there was a combination of status quo districts and a population growth well in excess of the national average. For, in Andrew Hacker's words, these states "are clearly in the midst of a social and economic upheaval, and the forces attracting migrants from the outside are also causing their own residents to move from old homes to new locations in the state." [6]

The case of Alabama is unique. In the post-1960 reapportionment the state lost one of its nine Representatives, a situation ordinarily guaranteed to produce a redistricting, since an election of so many representatives at-large is sufficiently unpredictable that state legislatures typically try to avoid it at all costs. The fact that Ala-

TABLE 9

*States that Gained or Lost Representation and Failed to Redistrict after 1960 **
(As of 1963)

Districts	*Population*	*Districts*	*Population*
ALABAMA		OHIO	
9 (Birmingham)	634,864	3 (Dayton)	726,156
7 (rural)	236,216	12 (Columbus)	682,962
MARYLAND		15 (small town)	236,288
5 (suburban Washington, D.C.)	711,045	TEXAS	
		5 (Dallas)	951,527
2 (Baltimore County)	621,935	20 (San Antonio)	687,151
		22 (Houston)	674,965
1 (rural)	243,570	4 (rural)	216,371
MICHIGAN			
16 (Detroit)	802,994		
12 (rural)	177,431		

* This table excludes one state, Hawaii, which gained one seat (in addition to its provisional Congressman under statehood admission) and chose to elect both Representatives at-large.

SOURCE: See Table 7.

bama is a one-party state made possible a provisional arrangement after a bitter battle between the legislature and governor resulted in an impasse. The rural "Black Belt," vastly overrepresented in the Alabama legislature, forced through a bill that would have reduced the state's congressional delegation to eight by "chopping up" metropolitan Jefferson county (Birmingham) into four parts and attaching them to adjoining rural districts. A gubernatorial veto suggested as an alternative a double primary plan whereby each of the nine existing districts would nominate one candidate, the first primary to be followed by a statewide run-off primary to select the top eight of the nine nominees. This plan was eventually passed at a special session. As expected, all nine incumbents were renominated in their own districts; after the run-off primary the top eight ran in the general election as the Democratic nominees (tantamount to election in this one-party state). Alabama is included in Table 9, even though technically all of its voters had an equal weight in the second primary and in the general election. Yet the existing districts so conditioned the nominating process that it seems appropriate to include it.

Tables 7, 8, and 9 clearly reveal a distinct pattern of increasing inequalities, in accordance with the conditions affecting each group of states. Where partial or complete redistricting took place after the 1960 census, the extremity of distortions was relatively low, even in the absence of express congressional requirements that districts be of approximately equal population.[7] Moreover, the balance between rural and small-town areas on the one hand, and urban and suburban communities on the other, was correspondingly more even in the states in Table 7. While there was some rural overrepresentation, there are sufficient exceptions to preclude a clearcut pattern. On the other hand, Tables 8 and 9 reveal not only greater inequalities in district populations, but a distinct rural-urban pattern as well. The overpopulated districts were typically urban or suburban, while the least populated ones were usually rural or small-town in nature.

From a national standpoint, the situation revealed by both action and inaction (but particularly the latter) of state legislatures on congressional redistricting added up to a considerable overall dilution of metropolitan strength in the House of Representatives. This imbalance can be most dramatically revealed by a comparison of the twenty most populous congressional districts with the twenty least populous after the reapportionment and redistrictings of 1961–1962 (see Table 10). The twenty most populous congressional districts, all metropolitan except for two (which had large suburban growth), claimed a total of 13,941,475 inhabitants—sufficient for virtually thirty-four Congressmen (based on the national population average per district). At the other extreme, the twenty least-inhabited districts, all rural or small-town in nature, held only 4,550,061 people, or the equivalent of eleven seats. This indicates a

TABLE 10

Twenty Largest and Smallest Congressional Districts after Reapportionment, 1960

	Largest Districts	Population	Nature of District		Smallest Districts	Population	Nature of District
1	Texas 5th	951,527	Metropolitan	1	Michigan 12th	177,431	Rural
2	Georgia 5th	823,680	Metropolitan	2	South Dakota 2nd	182,845	Small Town
3	Michigan 16th	802,994	Metropolitan	3	Colorado 4th	195,551	Rural
4	Ohio 3rd	726,156	Metropolitan	4	Arizona 3rd	198,236	Rural
5	Maryland 5th	711,045	Metropolitan	5	Texas 4th	216,371	Rural
6	Indiana 11th	697,567	Metropolitan	6	Alaska (at large)	226,167	Small Town
7	Michigan 18th	690,259	Metropolitan	7	Alabama 7th	236,216	Rural
8	Connecticut 1st	689,555	Metropolitan	8	Tennessee 8th	223,387	Rural
9	Texas 20th	687,151	Metropolitan	9	Oklahoma 3rd	227,692	Rural
10	Ohio 12th	682,962	Metropolitan	10	Tennessee 7th	232,652	Rural
11	Texas 22nd	674,965	Metropolitan	11	Ohio 15th	236,288	Small Town
12	Michigan 7th	664,556	Metropolitan	12	Wisconsin 10th	236,870	Small Town
13	Arizona 1st	663,510	Metropolitan	13	Florida 9th	237,235	Small Town
14	Florida 6th	660,345	Mid-urban	14	Michigan 11th	240,793	Rural
15	Colorado 2nd	653,954	Small Town	15	Florida 8th	241,250	Rural
16	Connecticut 4th	653,589	Metropolitan	16	Maryland 1st	243,570	Rural
17	Alabama 9th	634,864	Metropolitan	17	Texas 1st	245,942	Small Town
18	Tennessee 9th	627,019	Metropolitan	18	Texas 6th	248,149	Small Town
19	Michigan 6th	623,842	Metropolitan	19	Alabama 6th	251,765	Small Town
20	Maryland 2nd	621,935	Metropolitan	20	Oklahoma 4th	252,208	Rural

SOURCE: *Congressional Quarterly Special Report* ("Congressional Redistricting . . ."), *op. cit.* (September 28, 1962), p. 1604.

collective underrepresentation of about fourteen seats for the twenty most populous districts, with a consequent overrepresentation of nine for the corresponding group at the other end of the population scale.

These instances, of course, illustrate the extremes at both ends of the population spectrum. Any kind of composite picture would have to weigh the relative strength of the remaining congressional districts. Such an overall study was made by the Congressional Quarterly Service in 1962, showing the disparities revealed by applying the 1960 census figures to the old congressional districts before the new reapportionment. By classifying all districts into three categories—urban, suburban, and rural—this study computed the percentages of the nation's population in each and then applied these quotas to the total House membership. The result indicated that an "ideal" reapportionment would require a shift of twenty-seven seats away from rural areas, with twenty going to the suburbs and seven to central cities.[8] Some of these disparities were rectified by the redistricting actions in several states subsequent to the post-1960 reapportionment, though metropolitan areas were still considerably short of their proportionate share of strength. An analysis of all congressional districts (including those freshly drawn through 1962) classified in accordance with the four categories used so far in this chapter yielded the following comparative rating in terms of an "ideal" population standard:

Rural districts	11.6 seats overrepresented
Small-town districts	8.3 seats overrepresented
Mid-urban districts	2.0 seats underrepresented
Metropolitan districts	17.8 seats underrepresented

This indicated a distinct bonus of strength for rural and small-town areas at the expense of metropolitan communities, a grouping that includes both cities and suburbs. Of the two, the latter were clearly the major victims of underrepresentation.[9]

The situation just outlined, however, began to change as soon as the threat of court intervention in apportionment cases stimulated moves in many states for newly drawn congressional districts. The first successful result was produced by Wisconsin, which had not redrawn its congressional constituencies since 1931. A few months after *Baker v. Carr* was decided in 1962 a Federal district court dismissed "without prejudice" a challenge to the constitutionality of both congressional and legislative districts in Wisconsin. But the court left open the possibility of further litigation should the legislature fail to act during its 1963 session. After the state's Democratic governor and Republican legislature had engaged in several skirmishes (including a gubernatorial veto of one redistricting bill) the parties finally reached agreement in May, 1963 on an act providing new congressional districts. Then the Supreme Court's decision in *Wesberry v. Sanders* in February, 1964 set in motion still more redistricting activity among the states. By August of 1965 a total of eighteen states had redrawn congressional boundaries as a result of judicial pressure. These are listed in Table 11, revealing minimal or moderate disparities in population extremes in all of these states, quite a contrast with their prior figures. By the 1966 elections, under the terms of the redistricting legislation passed by the House of Representatives in March, 1965, all districts in the nation were to be brought within a population range of 15 percent above and 15 percent below a state's average.[10]

GERRYMANDERING. An additional important feature is gerrymandering, the time-worn art of maximizing the voting strength of the party in control by manipulating the district boundaries. The object of any gerrymander is to cause as many wasted opposition votes as possible, either by concentrating them in a few districts or spreading them as minority segments among many constituencies. Since one method of diluting the opposition's representative strength is to cause or to allow their

TABLE 11

Judicially Prompted Congressional Redistricting, 1963–1965

	Maximum Percentage Deviation from State Average		*Ratio of Most Populous to Least Populous District*	
State	1962	1965	1962	1965
Texas	128.5	9.8	4.4 to 1	1.2 to 1
Michigan	95.0	2.1	4.5 to 1	1.0 to 1
Georgia	108.9	16.4	3.0 to 1	1.4 to 1
Maryland	86.3	14.9	3.2 to 1	1.3 to 1
Ohio	79.5	18.1	3.1 to 1	1.3 to 1
Alabama	74.9	23.0	2.7 to 1	1.4 to 1
Indiana	64.6	12.8	2.4 to 1	1.2 to 1
Connecticut	63.2	14.1	2.2 to 1	1.2 to 1
*Florida	60.1	12.7	2.8 to 1	1.2 to 1
Tennessee	58.2	14.4	2.8 to 1	1.3 to 1
South Dakota	46.3	3.4	2.7 to 1	1.1 to 1
Colorado	55.4	12.6	3.3 to 1	1.2 to 1
Wisconsin	40.1	3.4	2.2 to 1	1.1 to 1
Oregon	40.0	8.4	2.0 to 1	1.2 to 1
*Arkansas	28.8	1.6	1.7 to 1	1.0 to 1
Utah	28.6	1.5	1.8 to 1	1.0 to 1
*Kansas	23.9	9.6	1.4 to 1	1.2 to 1
Idaho	22.9	9.4	1.6 to 1	1.2 to 1

* 1965 redistricting second since 1960 census.

SOURCE: Political Department, International Ladies' Garment Workers Union, August 12, 1965.

districts to be overpopulated, great disparities in district size frequently indicate either a positive or a "silent" gerrymander.

It is entirely possible, however, for a state to be divided equitably in terms of population, but with lines so drawn as to benefit the party or faction in control of the state legislature. An excellent example can be found in New York, where Republican legislatures in both 1951 and 1961 found it simple to gerrymander without unduly distorting congressional district populations. A classic case of "cartographical surgery" has been the persistent Republican effort to insure a safe GOP seat in overwhelmingly Democratic Brooklyn. The old twelfth district, created in 1951, tortuously twisted its way from one end of Brooklyn to the other, picking up widely scattered pockets of Republican strength to form a serpentine shape. Holding true to form, this district elected a Republican to Congress for four straight elections, but finally fell to the Democrats in 1960. New surgery was indicated, so in 1961 the Republican legislature designed the fifteenth congressional district in Brooklyn as safe GOP territory, producing a seahorse-shaped configuration which bears a striking resemblance to the original Gerrymander of 1812 (credited to Governor Gerry of Massachusetts).

Partisan manipulation in New York was not confined to this one instance, however. As the map of New York City congressional districts vividly illustrates (see Figure 1), the pattern of districting would do credit to a manufacturer of jigsaw puzzles. And while densely settled urban areas are typically most subject to the art of gerrymandering, New York Republicans also applied it to upstate areas; the thirty-fifth district, for example, extends almost two thirds of the way across the widest part of the state for some 200 miles.[11] Yet even the most skillfully designed plans of political technicians at times go awry. In 1962 New York Democrats survived the GOP gerrymander far better than anticipated, winning twenty of the state's forty-one congressional seats. Even the Brooklyn fifteenth district re-elected, by a narrow margin, the Democratic incumbent slated for "certain" defeat.

The pattern of congressional districts in New York was for years directly conditioned by a constitutional apportionment for the state house in Albany which virtually assured Republican dominance, regardless of the degree of statewide popular support. Thus Democrats had no realistic hope of capturing either branch of the legislature and had to rely entirely on the possibility of electing a governor who could bargain by the use or threat of a veto. These "rules of the game" now seem

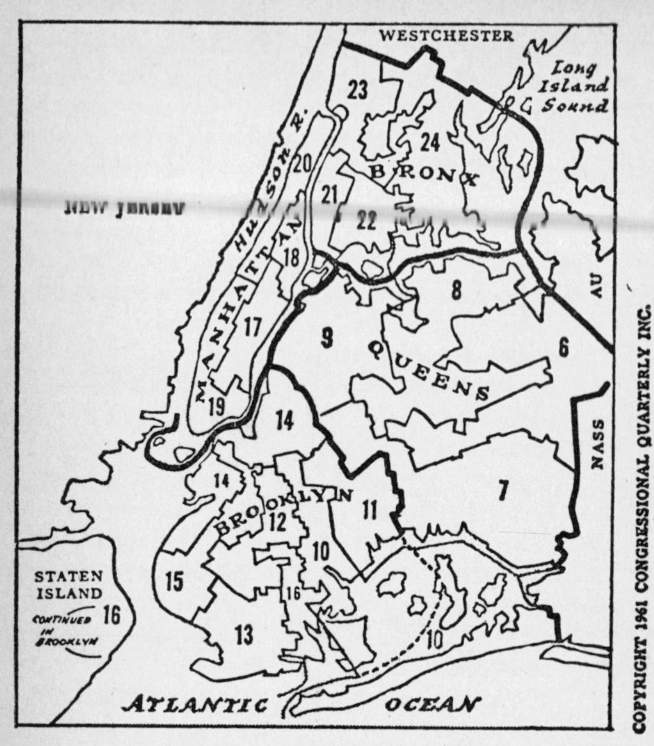

NEW YORK CITY DISTRICTS

destined to change as a result of judicial entry into the matter of legislative apportionment. New York's legislative districts were among those declared contrary to the Fourteenth Amendment's guarantees by the Supreme Court's historic decisions of June 15, 1964. The following month Governor Nelson Rockefeller called for a special session of the legislature to meet later in the year to revise the state's legislative districts. While New York's congressional constituencies survived an earlier challenge before the supreme tribunal, it is probable that future congressional districtings will be conditioned by closer two-party bargaining than previously.

In some other states a greater likelihood of party turnover has been present, since the geographic pattern of state districts has not necessarily placed either party in the role of a perpetual legislative minority. In this category, California offers an interesting example of gerrymanders by opposing parties after two successive post-census redistricting actions. In 1951 Republicans held the governorship and both houses of the California legislature, though they had a minority of registered voters. The resulting congressional redistricting gave the Republican party a disproportionately high share of the state's delegation for the next decade: [12]

Percent of	*1952*	*1954*	*1956*	*1958*	*1960*
Republican Congressional Vote	54.0	48.5	47.6	40.0	46.1
Republican Congressional Seats	63.3	63.3	56.6	46.7	46.7

Since the use of single-member districts tends to distort progressively upward the percentage of seats taken by the party gaining a majority of votes,[13] the above figures demonstrate a remarkable durability of the 1951 Republican gerrymander in California. The GOP was able to capture a majority of the delegation in 1954 and 1956 with a distinct minority of statewide votes. Only a combination of Democratic organization and voting power was able to cause a breakthrough, and then only a partial one. In fact, most of the Democratic gains occurred in nonmetropolitan areas where districts had been subject to little, if any, gerrymandering. Of twelve seats allocated to Los Angeles County in 1951, eight were designed as safe Republican districts, and the GOP lost only one [14] of these in a decade characterized by enormous population mobility, internal party strife, and a greatly strengthened Democratic opposition.

By 1961 the tables were turned and the Democrats held both houses of the state legislature in addition to the governor's office. The opportunity to re-gerrymander both the state assembly and congressional districts was sweetened by California's acquisition of eight new seats in Congress, the greatest absolute gain of any state. The new district map of 1961 revealed some definite advantages for the Democrats. For one thing, Republican districts were generally more populous, averaging 103.8 percent of the norm, while Democratic seats averaged 98 percent.[15] These averages obscure some substantial population disparities, with the most oversized and geographically contorted district (42 percent above the norm) a safe Republican one. In 1962 the Democrats gained nine congressional seats, while the Republicans lost one. With 52 percent of the popular vote, Democrats captured 66 percent of the state delegation. Yet Democratic gerrymandering was unable to avoid a large number of "wasted" votes for their own candidates as well as for Republicans. A perceptive explanation for this kind of situation can be found in Andrew Hacker's observation that outside the South, Democrats find it difficult to create many heavily populated Republican districts, because "except for a few well-to-do suburbs, fewer areas seem to attract Republicans en masse than Democrats." [16]

As might be expected, gerrymandering is facilitated when one party controls both houses of the legislature plus the governorship, as was true in New York and California in both 1951 and 1961. If there is any division in such control, then either bargaining between houses or the threat of a gubernatorial veto typically produces some compromises, as can be seen by the closely balanced delegations created in 1961 in Pennsylvania, New Jersey, Illinois, and Massachusetts. Thus, in two-party states, a party disadvantaged by the state apportionment system in one house can sometimes hope to capture the other, or failing that, the governorship. This is often more of a negative check on positive gerrymandering, however, and is of no avail when failure to redistrict is the cause of distortion and imbalance.

Even the existence of two-partyism helps moderate gerrymandering to some degree, since there are certain limitations imposed by the sheer numbers of the opposition, in addition to the unpredictability of population mobility in many areas. Moreover, fewer potentialities for gerrymandering exist in some states than in others. In general the more populous states with substantial metropolitan areas provide both greater stakes and more opportunities for manipulating districts for party advantage. In several states, especially smaller ones, there is little evidence of active gerrymandering. Also, voting behavior is sufficiently unpredictable in some areas to place added limits on the practice, while elsewhere (notably in western states) incumbency frequently has a stronger appeal than party designation. Furthermore, many redistrictings reveal a bipartisan type of gerrymander aimed at preserving incumbent Congressmen and minimizing the number of marginal districts. When this occurs, it mitigates some of the effects of gerrymandering.

In one-party states, on the other hand, the majority party is usually able to minimize any threat of opposition and frequently does so. In the Democratic South and the border states, the legislatures have been able to keep growing Republican strength well in check. For example, in Texas, Virginia, and Florida, urban and suburban Republicans have managed to elect Congressmen, but fewer than their numbers would indicate. The border state of Oklahoma is Democratic, but with a strong and growing Republican minority. Yet the state legislature has so far succeeded in corralling most Republican congressional strength in the state into an odd-shaped district that includes several northern rural counties before jutting down to take in barely adjoining (and Republican) Tulsa County.

The process of drawing district lines so as to minimize the opposing party's strength is often accepted as standard ground rules in American politics. Indeed, many state legislatures proceed to redistrict on the assumption that they have some sort of a popular mandate directing the victor to monopolize the spoils. Sometimes partisan leaders display a bold frankness in admitting and even boasting of gerrymandering. From a Missouri Democrat came this reply to Republican protests over the 1952 congressional districting there:

> Did the Republicans really expect the Democrats to draft and support a redistricting bill favorable to the Republicans? If they did their political training has been sadly neglected and their political acumen hovers near the zero mark. The Republicans are entitled to the same redistricting feast at the hands of the Democrats that they would serve the Democrats if they were in power. Only that—and nothing more.[17]

In a similar vein was the justification of the 1951 Republican gerrymander of New York. Senate majority leader Arthur Wicks said candidly:

> It would be hypocritical for me to deny that the bill may bring about an increased Republican representation in Congress. Of course, that is to be expected of legislation enacted by a Legislature which is controlled by the Republicans because the people of the state voted more Republicans than Democrats into the Legislature.[18]

These statements, though unusually frank, are fairly typical examples of the attitudes held by majority parties in state legislatures. Gerrymandering has been justified on the professed assumption that the "people" freely elected a legislature controlled by one party. Yet the unequal shares of strength that the "people" have long held in most state legislatures goes unmentioned. Even where the majority party does represent a true majority of the public, there are serious objections to allowing congressional redistricting to be treated entirely like a political plum. More than local partisan and sectional interests are involved in the result, since the whole fabric of national lawmaking is at issue.

This brief discussion of gerrymandering has indicated

the intimate relationship between the make-up of state legislatures and the partisan composition of congressional delegations, which in turn affects not only the total make-up of the Congress, but the intraparty balances as well. Districting patterns in the South and border states have favored rural and small-town Democrats at the expense of urban (and usually more liberal) Democrats, in addition to the heavy underrepresentation felt by Republicans in several southern states. In the northern and western states, positive or silent gerrymandering has tended to disadvantage suburban Republicans in particular, and city Democrats to a lesser degree. In the final analysis, it seems clear that the urban and suburban voters of both major parties had become significantly underrepresented on Capitol Hill by the time of the Supreme Court's insistence in 1964 that congressional districts be as equal in population as practicable. As for positive gerrymandering, it appears from the New York congressional case that the Court is reluctant to become involved so long as the districts are close to an equal standard of population.[19] Such reticence could change, however, if the courts should be charged with upholding standards of compactness and contiguity, as would presumably be the case under the redistricting legislation passed by the House of Representatives in 1965. This could help moderate at least the more grotesque geographic gerrymanders, though adroit forms of the practice will probably persist, with incumbent Congressmen of both parties continuing to receive special consideration. Further checks on gerrymanders may reasonably be anticipated in some states as their own legislatures are reapportioned and become more representative.

The Power Structure on Capitol Hill

Whatever numerical advantage may be held by rural and small-town districts in Congress is minor compared with the strategic advantages they enjoy in the actual power structure of each house. Public policy is less influenced by aggregate numbers than by strategically placed Congressmen who wield power far out of proportion to the size of the constituencies they represent. The more powerful congressional committees usually reflect a disproportionate rural and small town membership. Further, the most influential members, the committee chairmen, rise to their positions solely by virtue of seniority—a system that again works to the disadvantage of urban constituencies. Much positive legislation receiving both presidential and major-party support can easily be blocked by individuals or committees that are least reflective of and responsive to national public opinion.

The internal organization of both houses of Congress is characterized by thorough decentralization of power among numerous standing committees. The major decisions of legislative policy are made in the various committees, which generally hold the power of life or death for proposed statutes. Hence the very make-up of a committee is of crucial importance.

Within each committee the decisive role is played by the chairman, who in most cases can direct the legislative traffic as he sees fit. These powerful positions are allocated on the basis of seniority, with each party's committee membership ranked according to continuous service. For both parties the rise to power and influence is determined mainly by the ability to be re-elected. This system automatically places Senators and Representatives from "safe" states or districts at an enormous advantage. These "safe" constituencies for each party have usually been rural or small-town in nature. Fluid and changing metropolitan districts are more likely to be closely contested two-party areas that reflect more accurately newer and changing political tides. The seniority system favors those Congressmen who are least compelled to face strong competition on the basis of fresh issues. It renders a corresponding advantage to those economic interests that find support in the politically "safe" constituencies, where there is little chance of a turnover of representatives. Committee chairmen have traditionally been politicians whose own districts have remained insulated from any periodic transformations in the national political climate.

A glance at the committee rosters of either house of Congress will reveal a representative imbalance. In the Senate, seniority favors sectional minorities composed of less populous states. With the Democrats heavily in control of the upper house in 1963, Senators from the solid South chaired ten of the sixteen standing committees—a sizable amount of power for a section that elects but twenty-two of the Senate's 100 members. The remaining chairmen came largely from the Far West, a two-party area, but one where weak party organizations and nonpartisan voting habits tend to favor many incumbents. The only committee chairman from a heavily populated northern state was Senator McNamara of Michigan, who gained his position not from long seniority, which he did not have, but from the fortuitous circumstance of having begun on a less important and relatively noncoveted committee (Public Works).

On the other side of the Senate aisle, Republican ranking members were more diverse in locality, though nine of the sixteen minority leaders came from either New England or the Great Plains. Yet three of the more populous, industrial states—California, Illinois, and Massachusetts—could claim four ranking memberships. With no single large bloc of Senators from a one-party area, Republicans face somewhat fewer seniority hurdles than the Democrats. In the eighty-eighth Congress, the most senior Republican Senator had begun his service in 1941, and only four more prior to 1949. Democratic chairmen could date their seniority back to 1927, with a total of fifteen beginning prior to 1949. Both Democrats and Republicans from competitive, two-party states find it difficult to accumulate seniority in the upper house, and even those who do face periodic hazards of losing office entirely. In the recent past, defeat has reached such seemingly well-entrenched leaders as former Senators Bricker (Ohio), Capehart (Indiana), and Wiley (Wisconsin).

Due to its more parochial basis, the House of Representatives presents a somewhat different structure, in that most constituencies involved are geographic segments within states. Yet the pattern displays several similarities, with seniority again favoring those members from safe constituencies. As would be expected, such districts are usually located in areas that are relatively immune from population shifts (or, in some cases, ones that become more heavily one-party with added inhabitants of a particular socio-economic group). Table 12 reveals the distribution of chairmen and ranking minority members for the eighty-seventh and eighty-eighth Congresses.

TABLE 12

Distribution of House Chairmanships and Ranking Minority Members by Type of District

	87th Congress, 2nd Session (1962–1963)			88th Congress, 1st Session (1963–1964)		
	Demo.	*Repub.*	*Totals*	*Demo.*	*Repub.*	*Totals*
Rural	9	2	11	8	1	9
Small town	6	10	16	6	10	16
Mid-urban	1	5	6	2	4	6
Metropolitan	5	4	9	5	6	11
Totals	21	21	42	21	21	42

SOURCE: Adapted from tables in Thomas V. Martin, *Equal Representation and Congressional Districting: Urban and Rural Patterns of Political Power*, unpublished M.A. thesis, University of California, Santa Barbara, 1964, pp. 54, 58.

These figures suggest several points of interest. First of all, a large majority (close to 60 percent) of committee leadership positions were held by representatives from rural and small-town districts, which included approximately one third of the nation's inhabitants. The majority was even greater among Democratic chairmen only. Sectionally speaking, all but three of the rural and small-town Democratic chairmen came from the South, while their counterparts in the GOP were drawn entirely from the Midwest and East. Of the metropolitan representatives, Democratic chairmen were those from safe city districts (three in New York, one in Chicago, one in Oakland), while Republican ranking members in this category hailed from largely suburban areas in the Midwest and East.

Though positions of committee leadership still show a distinct rural and small-town preponderance, it should be noted that urban representation has been steadily increasing. A study of House committees in 1956 revealed that only five of the then thirty-eight chairmen and ranking members came from metropolitan districts.[20] Moreover, as Table 12 shows, the number of committee leaders from the cities and suburbs increased from nine to eleven in the span of just one session in 1963. One reason for this substantial improvement in urban status is the steady urbanization of the nation itself—more districts become urban each decade. (For example, after the 1960 census and subsequent reapportionment-redistrictings there were 175 metropolitan constituencies compared with 142 a decade earlier.) Also, while rural and small-town areas still tend to be "safer" for one party or the other, certain city districts show increasing population stability, allowing some metropolitan Democrats, in particular, a chance to accumulate seniority. At the same time, while suburbia continues to gain population swiftly, the type of growth in many places simply makes the districts safer for Republican incumbents.

In spite of these modifications, the committee structure in both houses of Congress still places a disproportionately large share of the nation's decision-making in the hands of individuals and groups least responsive to the felt needs of a modern industrialized society. An increasing amount of national legislation encompasses problems of primary concern to urban inhabitants—housing, civil defense, labor, and business policies, to mention a few. Yet the internal organization of Congress leaves that body inadequately equipped to handle these vital problems with real understanding. Furthermore, the local and unduly rural bias of Congress helps explain the wide gulf that so often separates the legislature from an executive branch inevitably more concerned with nationwide issues.

State Legislatures and Amending the Constitution

It is a well-established proposition that the process for amending the United States Constitution is extremely difficult. One intention of the framers, fearful of the "excesses of democracy," was to institute a check on the popular majority so that a change would require almost overwhelming support. As a result, constitutional growth since the eighteenth century has been largely accomplished by less formal means such as judicial review, the party system, and presidential powers.

The Constitution requires that amendments be proposed by a two-thirds vote of both houses of Congress or by a national convention called by Congress upon the application of legislatures in two-thirds of the states; proposed amendments must be ratified by three-fourths of the state legislatures or special conventions, whichever Congress decides upon. Due to the complexities of the procedure, only twenty-four amendments have been passed since 1789, and the first ten can be considered as virtually part of the original Constitution.

The amending process is still important, however, and the participation of the states is worthy of attention. Since state legislatures are in a position to petition Congress for amendments and are usually called upon to decide their ratification, the make-up of these bodies is once again important. While a preponderant popular sentiment may be desirable for basic changes in the governmental framework, the obvious question is: How well do state legislatures serve as barometers of public opinion?

The question of representation in state legislatures has frequently played an important role in the history of the national amending process. After the Civil War unsuccessful attempts were made to secure submission of the Thirteenth and Fifteenth Amendments to state conventions instead of to the legislatures, due to doubts concerning the representative nature of state lawmaking bodies. The rural-urban issue came to the fore during the campaign for prohibition of liquor, which resulted in the adoption of the Eighteenth Amendment in 1919. Most "dry" sentiment was located in rural areas, while cities were generally "wet." Spokesmen for the Anti-Saloon League publicly asserted that the proposed amendment must pass Congress before 1920, when a prospective reapportionment of the lower house in accordance with population changes would result in some forty new "wet" representatives.[21]

The only break with the tradition of allowing state legislatures to assume responsibility for ratification came with the repeal of the prohibition amendment. The "wets" had apparently not forgotten the importance of rural-dominated legislative bodies. Consequently the convention method was chosen by Congress as one that would allow a more representative opinion in the states.

Many believed that the adoption of the Twenty-first Amendment through the convention technique brought into vogue a more democratic ratification method. Congress nevertheless reverted to the process of state legislative ratification for the next three amendments.

The very nature of the amending process has acted as a barrier to attempted changes of a liberal nature. The large majorities needed both within Congress and among the states have allowed rural or sectional minorities to wield decisive vetoes. Recent trends, however, indicate that the difficulties are far fewer for conservative groups.

An interesting case in point is the recent attempt to limit severely the scope and extent of the Sixteenth (income tax) Amendment. The campaign apparently began in 1938 with the American Taxpayers Association, Inc., an offspring of the Committee for Constitutional Government. The purpose was to limit Federal income tax to a maximum of 25 percent on any amount of income. The effect would obviously be a marked shift in the tax burden from high-income groups to low-income groups. Congress, faced with the responsibility of obtaining adequate revenue for a large-scale budget, has shown little enthusiasm for an arbitrary ceiling on income taxation. Led in more recent years by the Western Tax Council, Inc. (with headquarters in Chicago), interests sponsoring the restriction found more responsive audiences in state legislatures.

By 1961 twenty-eight state legislatures had recommended to Congress the calling of a convention to limit the income tax, though several of these subsequently rescinded their actions. Consequently, no more than eighteen applications were validly pending.[22] While the income tax limitation campaign seems stymied, it serves as an interesting illustration of the extent to which a proposed basic change in public policy can win sponsorship from state legislatures with a minimum of publicity and debate. Since the predictable result of a rigid income tax ceiling would be higher taxes for most taxpayers, it seems unlikely that the measure, if understood, would receive the overwhelming support supposedly needed for a constitutional change.

A more recent attempt to originate constitutional amendments through state legislatures followed in the wake of the Supreme Court's 1962 reapportionment decision, *Baker v. Carr*. Late that same year the Council of State Governments initiated a movement to win state legislative sponsorship of three amendments to the United States Constitution. One proposed amendment would eliminate Federal court jurisdiction over the apportionment of state legislatures (in effect, reversing *Baker v. Carr*). Another would allow two thirds of the state legislatures to sponsor future amendments to the Federal Constitution without obtaining the approval of Congress for calling a convention, as presently required; instead there would be no convention, but merely a ratification process by three fourths of the state legislatures subsequent to sponsorship of an identically worded amendment by two thirds. The third proposal would establish a "Court of the Union," made up of the chief justices of the fifty states, with authority to review United States Supreme Court decisions on Federal-state relations.

By early 1963 the first two proposals had quietly won the approval of about a dozen legislatures and the third ("Court of the Union") of a handful, with passage of one or more of the resolutions in a single house completed in several other states. Then public notice was aroused, with newspapers, national wire services, and some law school professors calling attention to the "silent revolution." [23] The Chief Justice of the United States, Earl Warren, took the nation's lawyers to task for general silence about the amendments, suggesting that lack of discussion was virtually an abdication of the bar's responsibility to the public. Perhaps partly because of this prod, the American Bar Association's House of Delegates went on record against all three proposals in the summer of 1963. By the end of that year the drive had apparently lost its impetus. Yet the Supreme Court decisions on legislative apportionment in June of 1964 inspired moves in Congress to amend the United States Constitution so that one house of a bicameral state legislature need not reflect population.

Regardless of the outcome of any particular campaign to change the United States Constitution, the potential power held by state legislatures is sufficiently clear. While it was once assumed that Federal amendments required preponderant and highly active public support, such a generalization is now subject to revision, since it appears that certain types of moves for amendment may pass through many state legislatures almost without notice. Nor is this reversal so unusual as it may seem. Formerly most serious campaigns for constitutional amendments were progressive in nature, designed to remove or modify some of the restrictions on majority rule. More recently, since the Federal government has assumed a more active role in public policy, certain minority interests appear to seek protection in the amending clause. In such a situation, unrepresentative state legislatures provide an access to those groups that find less success at the national level.

In view of the impact of state legislatures on national institutions as well as on state and local policies, the time has clearly arrived for a much-needed reassessment of their adequacies. State lawmaking bodies claim moral authority to pass laws for public observance and otherwise act on behalf of the states' citizens. Their role then is—or should be—a representative one.

CHAPTER 6

One Man, One Vote: A Critique

The preceding chapters have described patterns of representation and their consequences at various levels of government. Yet underlying these institutional arrangements are values—both implicit and explicit—involving such questions as the proper interrelationship of governmental units and the reciprocal status of particular geographic interests within the larger political community. Legislative representation has been a perennial source of controversy throughout much of the nation. The recent entry of the Federal courts into the area of legislative apportionment has intensified the disputes over a number of basic issues. A reappraisal of some of the major concerns and values involved can furnish a perspective for many facets of the contemporary controversy.

Federalism and "States' Rights"

While the Supreme Court's 1964 apportionment decisions generated fresh debate over states' rights *vis-à-vis* the Federal judiciary, this was but one particular development in a broader re-examination of the American

Federal system. Quite apart from judicial intervention in the area of political rights, there had already existed for several years in some quarters a general concern over the proper scope and authority of Federal and state governments. Over the years several presidential commissions seriously studied the possibility of reversing the steady trend toward enlarged Federal responsibilities by reallocating certain powers to the states. Yet no such goals materialized, partly because the study commissions themselves realized their impracticality. It is not surprising that some urban spokesmen were skeptical about decentralization on the grounds that the terms "states' rights" and "local self-government" were far from synonymous. Many felt that a necessary condition for any shifting of powers was the attainment of more representative state governments. President Eisenhower's Commission on Intergovernmental Relations in 1955 came to the conclusion "that the more the role of the States in our system is emphasized, the more important it is that the State legislatures be reasonably representative of all the people."[1] Much the same sentiment was echoed in 1962 by the Advisory Commission on Intergovernmental Relations when it reported:

> No single feature of State government has been so vulnerable to criticism by statesmen and scholars alike as the unrepresentative situation into which many State legislatures have permitted themselves to drift. Few, if any, thoughtful State officials will deny that the States have brought upon themselves the present degree of judicial intervention in the reapportionment problem.[2]

The issue of states' rights must be viewed in a context of group interests and their varying degrees of influence on government. In the light of political patterns that have long prevailed at the state level, it is not surprising that some economic interests wished decisions to be made there rather than by agencies of the Federal government. State legislatures offered avenues of access and influence to groups that were far less powerful at the national level. Many past proposals to shift regulation of certain phases of economic life from Federal agencies to state governments meant in reality an abandonment or relaxation of controls. A diminishing reliance on the states' rights argument for this purpose seems likely in the future, as state legislatures—under judicial prodding—become more representative of their publics.

Localism and Community Interests

The defenders of unequal representation generally base their arguments on a number of implicit assumptions that bear re-examination. One of these regards localities, such as counties, as distinct communities of interest. It is asserted that legislative representation should recognize all of the various regions and communities in such a way that a few urban centers cannot dominate state political affairs. The so-called "balance" and "federal" plans, by which minority population areas are given control of one house while the other house more directly represents numbers, are usually defended as protecting all segments of the state's population against the majority. Yet this is a one-way argument. The proposition is never heard that heavily rural states should allow a small minority of cities to control one house of the legislature—a procedure that would be no more justified by democratic theory than the reverse, but that would follow from the logic of the "balance" concept. Giving area special consideration in one house while the other house represents population appears superficially to be a fair arrangement. Yet the central issue, beclouded by the nature of bicameralism, is obscured. The result of "balance" plans is that groups with less popular support gain an inordinate bargaining power, while measures having wide public support are as easily defeated in one house as two. Certainly it is clear that such "compromise" schemes have not resolved or avoided intense antagonisms in the states where they have operated.

The argument in favor of giving special recognition to various regions of a state through area representation often rests on the assumption that political boundaries conform to social or community boundaries. While this was largely true in the eighteenth century (and possibly later in some parts of the nation), it is hardly a tenable premise today. The early concept of representation assumed that representatives could actually speak for the small and highly homogeneous communities that then existed. A community was both a geographical and a socio-economic unit, with a high degree of autonomy and relatively little contact with other localities. Thus individual and regional interests could be considered as largely identical. This simple form of community has long since been displaced. The rapid and dynamic changes wrought by industrialization have ushered in new ecological patterns that scarcely parallel old political boundaries.

Surely it cannot be seriously suggested today that county or legislative districts typically correspond to distinct social communities. In nearly all cases political boundaries are necessarily arbitrary, drawn for the sake of convenience. Economic and social interests usually transcend county and even state lines. One glance at a map of the New York City metropolitan area reveals in dramatic fashion how artificial are state, county, and township boundaries in an area where natural ecological development has spread over parts of three states and numerous subunits of government. Similar situations exist, though not so dramatically, in all sections of the United States. While the disparity is especially noticeable for urban areas, even rural regions show little distinct correlation between political and social units. The doctrine of community interests is reminiscent of the theory set forth in the nineteenth century by John C.

Calhoun, who insisted that government must represent a majority of interests (assumed to be bounded by state lines) instead of numbers. What was brilliant in the abstract but out of touch with reality even in Calhoun's day is far less tenable in the complex urban society of the twentieth century.

If we disregard this formalistic attachment to political boundaries, however, we can and must recognize the genuine existence of localism in many areas. Its rationalization in terms of counties or towns often obscures a more understandable concern by relatively isolated communities that they have a voice in state government. It is hardly surprising that such localities insist that their interests cannot be adequately understood if they are lumped into a larger district, one perhaps dominated by other economic and political interests. Yet the argument frequently confuses representation with disproportionate political power. Many spokesmen who profess to want only a voice in policy-making for smaller counties actually want a veto power. It is often possible to accommodate the interests of many distinct communities without distorting the representative balance, though one must carefully define the meaning of community. The term cannot ordinarily apply to any locality with some sentiment for separate identity, though New Hampshire is possibly the exception that proves the rule. There, the ideal of substantially equal representation of both people and towns has long resulted in a lower house of 400 members, with the tiniest towns sending a part-time representative who serves one or more sessions out of every five. Without going to New Hampshire's extreme, other states may enlarge one or both houses in order to accommodate representative equality with a minimum of upset for incumbents and localities.

Some recognition of local political units was held permissible by the Supreme Court of the United States in its 1964 state apportionment decisions, so long as the policy is rationally based and does not result in any substantial distortion of statewide representative equality. Chief Justice Warren expressed the Court's view in these words:

> A state may legitimately desire to maintain the integrity of various political subdivisions, insofar as possible, and provide for compact districts of contiguous territory in designing a legislative apportionment scheme. Valid considerations may underlie such aims. Indiscriminate districting, without any regard for political subdivisions or natural or historical boundary lines, may be little more than an open invitation to partisan gerrymandering. . . .
>
> . . . So long as the divergences from a strict population standard are based on legitimate considerations incident to the effectuation of a rational state policy, some deviations from the equal-population principle are constitutionally permissible with respect to the apportionment of seats in either or both of the two houses of a bicameral State Legislature.[3]

This statement indicates a realistic attempt to make room for the genuine interests of local communities so long as any resulting deviations are incidental to a general pattern of population equality. But the supreme tribunal emphasized once more its basic guideline that "the overriding objective must be substantial equality of population among the various districts, so that the vote of any citizen is approximately equal in weight to that of any other citizen in the state." [4]

Majority Rule and Minority Rights

The Supreme Court's apportionment decisions have focused fresh attention on some of the basic questions of representative democracy. One issue that has long been at the heart of the whole controversy over representative equality is the relationship of majority rule to minority rights. Defenders of rural overrepresentation usually assert that less-populated areas deserve proportionately greater influence as a means of protecting themselves against a tyrannical urban majority. It is quite true that democratic theory is concerned with minority rights as well as majority rule. Yet does the protection of minorities necessitate yielding either control or a veto power to them? If so, then the traditional principles of majority rule must be abandoned.

Furthermore, the case for rural minority rights rests on an assumption that cities constitute, singly or in combination, a cohesive political force. Yet does this square with reality? Do all, or even most, urban centers in a state function as unanimous forces in the body politic? Experience indicates a negative answer. After all, cities are divided on political matters; none constitutes a single and distinct group in regard to social and economic policies. The fears expressed over possible city domination of legislative bodies betray an inadequate understanding of the nature of modern society.

Nor are defenders of rural power alone in oversimplifying the problem. Indeed, the traditional case in favor of equal representation also envisages the issue in terms of a majority-minority dichotomy that by itself is now inadequate and misleading. When Jefferson protested in the eighteenth century against a system of representation in which "every man in Warwick has as much influence in the government as seventeen in Loudon" he spoke the language of classical individualism. In that day such an approach seemed to make good sense. It was assumed that there was a direct connection between each "political man" and his representative and that his weight in the political process could be measured in terms of individual interests. The ideal of political equality was naturally translated into the corollary principle of equal representation. This orientation has likewise characterized, to a large extent, the traditional analyses by political scientists and others interested in the problem of representation. The assertion that one person in county A has four, six, or thirty times the weight of each person in county B is still a telling point.

But the complexity of the political process, especially in the twentieth century, calls for a re-examination of some of the premises underlying former theories. A realistic approach to the problem of representation today must go beyond the terminology of individualism and consider the relevance of group relationships in the political process. The principle of equal representation still merits a solid justification, but for reasons that must be stated in different terms from those of eighteenth- and nineteenth-century political theorists.

If we regard society in terms of group interests we can approach the question of majorities and minorities more meaningfully. The so-called urban majority is simply an aggregate of people representing any number of distinct (and often politically antagonistic) groups. It was observed earlier that some urban business interests make political alliances with certain rural forces rather than with other urban interests. This is just one indication of important group cleavages. While rural society is usually more homogeneous, it too has important internal differences. For instance, in many states there is a variance in broad political outlook between farmers and the rural small-town elements, though courthouse "rings" of the latter usually monopolize political leadership for the whole area.

While public policy is consequently the result of multigroup pulls and pressures, the concrete legislative issues involved must be decided in terms of majorities and minorities within the lawmaking body itself. In this sense it is true that on certain questions more urban representatives may take a different position from that of most rural legislators. This stage, however, is only the final one in a complex process and tends to obscure earlier negotiations reached as a result of the political power pattern. Furthermore, as regards actual cohesiveness, legislators from the countryside and small towns have a widespread reputation for a far higher degree of solidarity than those representing cities, where articulate group interests are more diversified. In some states a high degree of urban solidarity might be expected on particular municipal problems as distinguished from broad, statewide social and economic issues. For instance, there could conceivably be an "urban bloc" on such matters as grants-in-aid to cities, home rule, local tax powers, and the like (though many mayors complain that even here unity among urban legislators is lacking). In such a situation it seems logical that urban areas should have a proportionate voice. It is true that an urban majority in this sense might abuse its powers just as any majority might. But the answer hardly seems to be minority rule and potential abuse.

Moreover, viewing the question of legislative representation from the standpoint of rural or sectional minorities unduly narrows the definition of minority to the criterion of area. There are more than just geographic minorities in all states (not to mention the diverse minority interests within such geographic areas); there are occupational, ethnic, religious, economic, racial, and a host of other minorities in our society. Is it not as logical to insist on safeguarding these minority interests through extra representation as it is to justify an apportionment that purports to protect the rights of minority geographic areas? Indeed, some systems of legislative representation that have been defended as protecting the rights of rural minorities have actually worked to the disadvantage of urban-based minorities. A case in point was the situation in several southern states, where inflated rural control for many years diluted the political influence of the Negro minority, which achieved a greater degree of suffrage in the urban areas with less political weight.[5]

In a pluralistic society, characteristic of the United States, any majority is simply an aggregate—often temporary—of minority groupings. The "urban majority" is in reality a coalition of many minority interests. Indeed, recognition of this fact makes the whole constitutional status of representative equality more understandable. When the Supreme Court entered the field of legislative apportionment it invoked the equal protection clause of the Fourteenth Amendment—a provision typically concerned with minority rights rather than majority rule. Thus judicial vindication of the so-called urban majority is in reality a recognition of the right to proportionate political power for a kaleidoscopic configuration of diverse minority interests which, in the aggregate, comprise an "urban majority."

Majority rule must be understood as the end product of political freedoms, including the free access of various minorities to combine and elect a majority government. In a democracy any such majority is limited by the constitutional status of minorities to equal political and social freedoms. When we regard minority rights in this basic sense, we do not ordinarily look for their protection in institutional veto powers; we typically rely on such safeguards as political self-restraint and, if necessary, the courts. As Chief Justice Warren reminded us in the historic 1964 apportionment decisions: "Our constitutional system amply provides for the protection of minorities by means other than giving them majority control of State Legislatures." [6]

The Fear of Urban Tyranny

The complexity of the situation renders the chance of "urban tyranny" highly improbable if equal representation did exist. In those few states, such as Massachusetts, Wisconsin, and Oregon, where equitable urban-rural representation has prevailed in modern times there has been no evidence that legislators representing urban majorities have acted in concert to exploit the rest of the state. In most states there is a degree of rivalry among cities in addition to the differences within each of them. For example, San Francisco and Los Angeles can hardly be expected to send delegations solidly allied with each other to the California legislature; and within each city are party, factional, social, economic, and other differences that hardly comprise one big urban interest. In the few instances where one urban area contains a majority of the state population, there is likewise no reasonable ground for believing that this center would—or, indeed, could—act as a single organic entity in "controlling" the legislature. Such a fear overlooks the complexity of political and social structure that is particularly evident in metropolitan areas. The professed apprehensions of downstate Illinois at the possibility of Cook County "domination" are groundless in view of the marked difference in social and political outlook between the city of Chicago and the suburban area of the county, to mention one obvious cleavage.

While a granting of urban representation proportionate to population would not result in a single, cohesive urban majority, it could effectuate a considerable shift in the pattern of political power. Some urban interests that formerly had little influence would probably gain more, while others (notably those that enjoy an advantage from an alliance with rural forces) would lose some. It is this potential shift in the power equilibrium that arouses the greatest resistance from the elements benefiting from the status quo. That resistance is prompted by a fear not of *an* urban interest, but of *certain* urban interests.

An imbalance of representative strength, then, means that accessibility to the decision-making process is rendered difficult or impossible for some groups and easier for others. Interests that have greater influence in constituencies with inflated power possess an obvious advantage over those whose support comes from areas that are underrepresented. Jefferson's classic example ("every man in Warwick has as much influence as seventeen in Loudon") translates into contemporary terms something like this: those interests with influence in Warwick have an advantage over those interests whose support is confined to Loudon. But in spite of a change in terminology, equal representation is as essential to modern democracy as it was in an earlier day. Only under such a system can governmental structure be considered as allowing all significant groups a potentially equal degree of accessibility to the decision-making process.

CHAPTER 7

The Judicial Revolution

By the middle of the twentieth century the prospects for representative equality both in state legislatures and in the national House of Representatives seemed remote indeed. In the face of legislative failure to reapportion, the passage of time resulted in greater and greater disparities from the ideal of "one man, one vote." In those states where constitutions were the main cause of representative imbalance, change usually depended upon amendments proposed by the legislatures themselves—the bodies least hospitable to such a shift in political power. An alternative method of securing a change in apportionment—the convening of a constitutional convention—was not generally a practicable answer, since legislatures were typically reluctant to authorize them. In fact, the fear of possible changes in apportionment patterns has been a basic underlying reason for the widespread failure of states to hold conventions for much-needed general constitutional revision. Georgia's constitution of 1945 was drawn up by an appointed commission whose work was subject to legislative revision before being submitted to popular vote. No constitutional change by the convention method seemed possible due to legislative fear of a popularly based group which might tamper with representation or the county-unit system. New Jersey secured a new constitution in 1947, after years of agitation, only when the legislature authorized a "limited" convention which was prohibited at the outset from even discussing the question of legislative representation.[1] But in many other states constitutional conventions, even if called into being, offered little hope of reform, since they would typically be based on existing legislative districts and would thus reflect the same malapportionment. This explains the long opposition by Michigan Democrats to a convention until the representative basis of such a body was changed.

Reapportionment by Popular Initiative

The only institutional process which seemed to offer potential for creating more representative legislatures was the initiative petition—available in a minority of states. Thirteen states include the initiative as part of the constitutional amending process as well as for direct legislation, while seven others restrict the initiative to legislation only. By 1963, six states had employed this direct device to alter apportionment patterns—in some cases in the direction of more representative equality, in others, in the opposite.

Examples of more representative reapportionments by initiative include two statutes in Washington state (1930 and 1956) and a constitutional amendment in Oregon in 1952.[2] This latter measure also included farsighted enforcement provisions by placing the duty of decennial reapportionment with the secretary of state in the event of legislative failure, with an added guarantee of judicial review.

On the other side of the ledger were reapportionments by constitutional initiative in California (1926) and Michigan (1952), both of which abandoned original constitutional provisos for senate representation on a population basis. Interestingly, in both of these highly urbanized states, the initiative propositions received substantial support from urban voters. Moreover, in each case the electorate chose the less representative plan in preference to an alternative population-based initiative on the same ballot. Once established, the California senate survived unsuccessful attempts at modification by initiatives in 1948, 1960, and 1962.[3]

Two other states have recorded mixed results. In Arkansas the constitutional initiative was employed in 1936 after nearly a half century of legislative failure to reapportion. The successful amendment transferred the decennial function from the legislature to a board of reapportionment, vesting in the state supreme court the power to review and, if necessary, revise abuses of discretion by the board. In 1956, however, the Arkansas Farm Bureau Federation sponsored a successful initiative that froze the senate districts as laid out (on the basis of 1950 population) by court order in 1952. Finally, in 1932 Colorado's electorate passed a statutory initiative establishing population ratios for both houses. But thirty years later this state's voters had a choice between two constitutional amendments, one of which would have created a commission to apportion both houses periodically on a population basis. This plan was rejected in favor of the alternative amendment, which called for a population-based lower house and a senate frozen substantially along the lines of the pre-existing apportionment. The Colorado plan was one of the six legislative apportionments invalidated by the Supreme Court's historic set of decisions on June 15, 1964.

While the initiative process (prior to judicial intervention) has served as the most effective potential remedy for legislative failure to reapportion, its limitations were—and are—many. This direct device is limited to a minority of states, and in some of these its use is modified. In others there are procedural barriers. For example, in Ohio petitions must contain signatures totaling 10 percent of the previous vote for governor and be so distributed that in at least half the state's counties 5 percent of the voters sign the petitions. Some states allow legislative amendment or revision of direct legislation, a power invoked by lawmakers in the state of Washington to restore most former districts after the electorate's favorable vote on the 1956 reapportionment initiative.[4]

Even in states where the initiative is used fairly extensively, it is a cumbersome and usually expensive operation, however useful it has often been. Its past success in providing more representative legislatures in a few states has typically depended upon a broad base of support, including at least some endorsement by the urban press. Bipartisan backing has been a source of strength, but this would obviously be difficult to obtain in those states where one party has a stake in the status quo.

Moreover, electorates in some states, as noted, have approved highly unequal apportionment measures sponsored by an initiative. So the question then remains whether the right to representative equality should necessarily depend upon the discretion of a majority of voters. As we shall see later, the Supreme Court of the United States specifically addressed itself to this question in its landmark state apportionment decisions of 1964.

Judicial Nonintervention

In view of the paucity of remedies available for effective and realistic resolution of the problem of unequal legislative representation, it is hardly surprising that disadvantaged individuals and interests should turn to the courts. As the perceptive French visitor to America, Alexis de Tocqueville, noted in 1835, "Scarcely any political question arises in the United States that is not resolved, sooner or later, into a judicial question."[5]

State courts have long exercised jurisdiction to pass upon the validity of legislative reapportionments, but have usually interpreted the separation of powers doctrine as prohibiting the judiciary from attempting to force positive action by the legislature. Though holding reapportionment to be a clear and mandatory legislative duty, state tribunals typically came to the unhelpful conclusion that "the people have no remedy save to elect a General Assembly which will perform that duty." [6] State courts restricted themselves to striking down gross malapportionments, which merely perpetuated the prior unequal districting patterns. Since either constitutional formulas or legislative inaction were the most common causes of representative inequality, this negative judicial role offered little relief. Courts could act positively only in those few states, such as Oregon and Arkansas, where the constitutions specifically involved the judiciary in the process of reapportionment.

Failing state remedies, dissatisfied citizens on occasion turned to Federal courts, again without success until recent years. In 1931 a Federal appeals court denied the contention of a Chicago resident that the United States Government had failed to guarantee a republican (that is, representative) form of government in Illinois. Several other suits challenged congressional districts within states. While Federal courts accepted jurisdiction here, they did not attempt to force state legislatures to create congressional districts equitably.[7] Then, in 1946 the issue came to a head when the Supreme Court of the United States handed down its decision in *Colegrove v. Green*. Here urban voters in Illinois challenged the population inequalities (ranging from 112,116 to 914,653) in congressional districts that had remained unchanged since 1901. The petitioners contended that their votes were diluted by sharing them with so many others and were thus worth far less proportionately than those of voters in the state's less populous districts. This attack on the status quo relied especially upon Article I, Section 2, of the United States Constitution, in addition to the Fourteenth Amendment's guarantees of due process and equal protection of the laws.

An undermanned Supreme Court held against Colegrove and his fellow challengers by a vote of 4 to 3, with the majority split on the reasoning. Writing the prevailing opinion, Justice Felix Frankfurter declared that the type of case presented was not a matter for judicial determination, concluding with the futile suggestion that "the remedy for unfairness in districting is to secure State legislatures that will apportion properly, or to invoke the ample powers of Congress." [8] Frankfurter insisted that the case was of a "peculiarly political nature" and that it would be "hostile to a democratic system to involve the judiciary in the politics of the people." [9] And for several years other judges were to echo Frankfurter's warning that "courts ought not to enter this political thicket." [10] A concurring opinion by Justice Wiley Rutledge expressed the view that the issues were judiciable, but that the Court should decline to exercise its jurisdiction because of several matters, including the proximity of forthcoming congressional elections.

Speaking for the three-man minority in the *Colegrove* case, Justice Hugo Black contended that both the equal protection clause of the Fourteenth Amendment and Article I of the Constitution forbade the kind of representative inequality found in Illinois. A state, he insisted, would not be permitted to pick out one group of citizens and deny them the vote altogether, or expressly to allot a half vote for some citizens and a full vote for others. Yet grossly unequal apportionments have the same effect. It was a mere "play upon words," Black continued, to term such a controversy "political" in the sense that "courts have nothing to do with protecting and vindicating the right of a voter to cast an effective ballot." [11]

In retrospect, it is puzzling that a case evoking such a

variety of opinions from a closely divided and undermanned supreme tribunal should so readily become a general precedent for the doctrine of judicial nonintervention in legislative apportionment. Yet such was the result for both congressional and state cases. And a subsequent decision in 1950 in *South v. Peters* upheld the Georgia county unit system, which projected inequalities in the legislature to the statewide and congressional primary elections. At this point the prospects seemed dim for those advocating more representative political institutions. While the precedents were of recent vintage and stemmed from divided courts, surely few would have been so sanguine as to anticipate a change of direction as early as 1962.

The Road to Judicial Intervention

An understanding of the Supreme Court's willingness to enter the "political thicket" of legislative apportionment must begin with a recognition of a more general shift in the high tribunal's own concept of its role in the American governmental system.[12] While it has been vastly overemphasized by his critics, who find a single scapegoat a simple convenience, the appointment of Earl Warren as Chief Justice in 1954 did symbolize new leadership; the naming of Warren, together with other later appointments, resulted in a Supreme Court that generally reflected fresh perspectives and a more active concept of the judiciary's role than was characteristic of the preceding tribunal, led by Chief Justice Fred Vinson. The school desegregation decisions of 1954 and subsequent determinations in other areas made clear the high court's willingness to take a more vigorous interpretation of the Fourteenth Amendment's equal protection clause.

The first sign of a possible re-examination of judicial noninvolvement in legislative apportionment came in 1956 from a Federal district court in Hawaii, which refused to dismiss a complaint against the territorial legislature's long failure to reapportion seats. Since this was a territorial case it did not involve the Fourteenth Amendment, but an equivalent appeal was made on the equal protection clause of the Congressional Organic Act establishing the territory, plus the Fifth Amendment's due process clause. While not a directly applicable precedent for state cases, the decision in *Dyer v. Kazuhisa Abe* is of interest both for its reasoning and its sweeping language. Stressing the recent segregation decisions, Judge Frank McLaughlin contended: "A classification which discriminates geographically has the same result. It deprives the citizen of his constitutional rights. Reasons of delicacy should no longer stay the judicial hand. . . . Any distinction between racial and geographic discrimination is artificial and unrealistic; both should be abolished." Finally, the opinion concluded with a stirring plea for judicial activism:

> The time has come, and the Supreme Court has marked the way, when serious consideration should be given to a reversal of the traditional reluctance of judicial intervention in legislative reapportionment. The whole thrust of today's legal climate is to end unconstitutional discrimination. It is ludicrous to preclude judicial relief when a mainspring of representative government is impaired. Legislators have no immunity from the Constitution. The legislatures of our land should be made as responsive to the Constitution of the United States as are the citizens who elect the legislators.[13]

The district court in Hawaii did not actually have an opportunity to fashion a remedy, since Congress passed an amendment to the Organic Act specifying a new legislative apportionment. But some of the passionate *obiter dicta* in this case were to appear in later apportionment cases.

By this time interested groups in several states, encouraged by the willingness of the Supreme Court to reexamine other controversial areas of judicial doctrine, began to press legal attacks on malapportionment. In 1958 a group of urban voters in Minnesota challenged their legislature's refusal to redistrict since 1913. Asserting that their federal rights had been violated, the petitioners asked a Federal district court to require at-large elections for the legislature for that year's primary and general elections. The court accepted jurisdiction and noted the factual data of inequality that had arisen in the preceding forty-five years due to legislative failure to reapportion. But the court then postponed a decision on the merits until the state legislature had one more opportunity to deal with the question.[14] Since the Federal court retained jurisdiction, the legislators could not afford to ignore the indirect threat. The lawmakers struggled with the issue of redistricting for nearly four months of the regular 1959 session and another seven weeks in special session before finally passing the state's first reapportionment act in forty-six years. While falling short of the state constitution's population standard for both houses, it was a substantial step in that direction and augmented considerably the legislative power of urban areas.

In 1960 a unique case, involving both geographic gerrymandering and racial discrimination, arose in Alabama. Fearful of the growing Negro voting potential in Tuskegee, the Alabama legislature redrew the city boundaries in a strangely irregular pattern which removed from the former city virtually all Negro voters and placed them in the county where their strength was easily absorbed by white voters. A challenge by Negroes was unsuccessful in lower courts, which upheld the state's action on the basis of well-established precedents allowing state governments to change boundaries of political subdivisions without judicial inquiry into motives.

The Supreme Court of the United States unanimously reversed the lower court judgment in this case, *Gomillion v. Lightfoot*. It was clear in both earlier oral argument as well as in the written opinions that the justices were concerned about the implications of the case for other types of gerrymanders.[15] Justice Frankfurter wrote the opinion for the Court. As the author of the prevailing opinion in *Colegrove v. Green,* he was particularly sensitive about the dangers of undermining his earlier handiwork and took great pains to distinguish the two cases as having nothing in common:

> While in form this is merely an act redefining metes and bounds, if the allegations are established, the inescapable human effect of this essay in geometry and geography is to despoil colored citizens, and only colored citizens, of their theretofore enjoyed voting rights. That was not *Colegrove v. Green.*[16]

Frankfurter's apparent concern about opening up the broader question of geographic gerrymanders led him to rest the *Gomillion* decision on the Fifteenth Amendment's guarantee against racial restrictions on the right to vote rather than the Fourteenth Amendment's equal protection clause. Yet this posed some awkward problems. Tuskegee Negroes who were registered could still vote in state and county elections, so their franchise had not actually been removed. The right to vote had not been assumed to include the right to be a resident in a particular subunit of government. For reasons such as these, Justice Charles B. Whittaker felt that the state's action was not in conflict with the Fifteenth Amendment, but rather violated the equal protection clause of the Fourteenth Amendment. His concurring opinion insisted that Alabama's action in "fencing Negroes out" of Tuskegee was an illegal segregation of races. Justice William O. Douglas separately concurred with the Court's opinion, but recorded his adherence to his former dissents in *Colegrove v. Green* and *South v. Peters.*

The cases just discussed suggest the increased frequency of legal challenges to apportionment patterns during this period. In several instances lower courts were less bold and experimental than those in Minnesota and Hawaii. But the awakening interest in the problem in many parts of the nation reflected a sense that the time might be at hand when the Supreme Court would reconsider the doctrine of nonintervention.

Baker v. Carr

One week after deciding *Gomillion v. Lightfoot* the Supreme Court agreed to review the Federal district court decision in *Baker v. Carr.* The case resulted from attempts during the 1950's by urban voters in Tennessee to challenge their state legislature's failure since 1901 to adjust constituencies in accordance with population changes. The state constitution required that both houses be based on population (with only a slight modification in one house). But each decade the gap between constitutional theory and institutional fact had increased. Studies revealed that about two thirds of the senate could be controlled by 37 percent of the population, while the same share of the lower house represented 40 percent of the voters. Population shifts had been typically uneven and there were strange disparities in representative strength even among the smaller rural counties. State courts had condemned both the inequalities and the legislature's failure to live up to its constitutional obligation, but had declined to intervene. There existed no institutional means of circumventing the legislature (such as the initiative, or a periodic referendum for a constitutional convention).

When the plaintiffs next turned to the Federal district court they won a sympathetic acknowledgment that their rights had indeed been violated; but their suit was dismissed on the ground that the remedy did not lie with the courts. Invoking *Colegrove v. Green* for support, the three-judge lower court concluded that "federal courts, whether from a lack of jurisdiction or from inappropriateness of the subject matter for judicial consideration, will not intervene in cases of this type to compel legislative apportionment."[17]

The importance of the Tennessee apportionment appeal is indicated by the fact that the Supreme Court heard oral argument during the 1960 term and then scheduled reargument during the 1961 term. Much deliberation must have preceded the history-making decision handed down on March 26, 1962. Altogether the six separate opinions totaled 165 printed pages of reports. Justice William J. Brennan, Jr., wrote the opinion of the Court for the six-man majority. There were three separate concurring opinions in addition to the two dissents by Justices Frankfurter and Harlan (one member of the tribunal, Justice Whittaker, was ill and did not participate).

The main legal point of the *Baker* case was the ruling that apportionment suits were judiciable. The Court emphasized that a majority of the seven-man bench deciding *Colegrove v. Green* had actually held in favor of this point (since Justice Rutledge's concurrence was based on other grounds; on judiciability he agreed with the three dissenters). Moreover, the Court in *Baker v. Carr* indicated that some apportionments could be so unfair as to violate the Fourteenth Amendment's equal protection of the laws clause. But it declined to specify the degree of malapportionment necessary to violate that guarantee. Even the Tennessee apportionment was not specifically invalidated; the case was sent back to the Federal district court to decide whether the state's districting pattern was unconstitutional.

The fervent dissenting opinion of Justice Frankfurter made an eloquent plea for the doctrine of judicial self-restraint as espoused by his earlier opinion in the *Colegrove* case. His lengthy and elaborate dissent serves as a fitting valedictory, for illness removed him from participation a few weeks later and caused his retirement before the following term. Frankfurter warned that the decision could well impair the Court's position as the ultimate interpreter of the supreme law of the land. He continued: "The court's authority–possessed neither of the purse nor the sword–ultimately rests on sustained public confidence in its moral sanction," [18] a quality nourished by complete judicial detachment from political entanglement. Finally, in a pithy passage that neatly sums up the essence of his judicial philosophy, Frankfurter contended:

> There is not under our Constitution a judicial remedy for every political mischief, for every undesirable exercise of legislative power. The Framers carefully and with deliberate forethought refused so to enthrone the judiciary. In this situation, as in others of like nature, appeal for relief does not belong here. Appeal must be to an informed, civically militant electorate. In a democratic society like ours, relief must come through an aroused popular conscience that sears the conscience of the people's representatives.[19]

The obvious query to this assertion is: How can this conscience of the people's representatives be seared when it is not accountable to a majority of the electorate? Frankfurter's philosophy of judicial noninvolvement, as expressed earlier in his *Colegrove* opinion, brought this appraisal from Professor Alpheus Mason: "Such deference to the legislature illustrates the logical inconsistency of the application of judicial self-restraint in cases affecting political rights. To say that the only remedy lies with the body that perpetuates the abuse is to admit that there is no remedy." [20]

As was indicated in the first chapter, the diverse opinions of the majority in *Baker v. Carr* gave little concrete direction to lower courts except for the generalization that the Fourteenth Amendment stands as a bar to some types of representative inequality. Some commentators criticized the Court for laying down no more specific guidelines for lower courts to follow. Yet this may have been a calculated and perceptive move. By letting state and lower Federal courts tackle the specific problems in particular states, the supreme tribunal would be able to gauge the reactions—both political and judicial—before moving farther. If this was the case, the nine men of the high court must have been impressed with the ensuing flood of litigation, with the largely favorable tone of public and newspaper reaction, and with the dispersed and fragmented nature of the political opposition. Finally, there was the alacrity with which many lower court judges moved to correct alleged malapportionments, seeming to reflect a welcome shouldering of responsibility on an issue that had earlier seemed virtually without a remedy. And while these lower court judges often proceeded tentatively and reached diverse results, the general pattern was clearly in favor of more representative legislatures.

As for the Supreme Court itself in this interim period, it decided only one case during its 1962 term that had a bearing on the apportionment problem. In March, 1963 the Court held in *Gray v. Sanders* that the Georgia county unit system violated the Fourteenth Amendment's equal protection clause. The old system, which projected a severe degree of legislative malapportionment into statewide primary elections, had already been invalidated by the Federal district court. But the lower court would allow a new unit system provided that the disparities in the electoral strength of counties were no greater than that of states in the Federal Electoral College. The 1962 Democratic primary had already taken place simply by counting ballots on an equal basis with no regard to county units. Now the Supreme Court declared that the attempted analogy to the Electoral College which would have allowed a newer and less inequitable system was inapposite. Speaking for the Court, Justice William O. Douglas emphasized the point that the case before it did not involve legislative representation:

Once the geographical unit for which a representative is to be chosen is designated, all who participate in the election are to have an equal vote—whatever their race, whatever their sex, whatever their occupation, whatever their income, and wherever their home may be in that geographical unit.[21]

Justice Douglas concluded on a broader note, however, which was to serve as useful *obiter dicta* in future apportionment cases: "The conception of political equality from the Declaration of Independence, to Lincoln's Gettysburg address, to the Fifteenth, Seventeenth, and Nineteenth Amendments can mean only one thing—one person, one vote." [22] In spite of the Court's disclaimer of suggesting anything of relevance to pending or future cases involving legislative representation, Justice Harlan centered his dissent around the fear that the decision was at least the entering wedge.

The 1964 Decisions

In November, 1963, the Supreme Court heard oral argument for over seventeen hours (nearly a week of argument time) on the appeals from six states. Congressional districts were at issue from Georgia and New York, while state legislative district patterns were contested in Alabama, Maryland, Virginia, and New York. (Oral argument was scheduled for Delaware the following month and for Colorado in March, 1964.)

Since the Court's decision in the *Baker* case had left the substantive issues unresolved, many looked to the lengthy period of oral argument for some signs of the justices' mood and the direction in which the nine men might move. Two Justices, Byron White and Arthur Goldberg, had been appointed since the earlier apportionment decision, replacing retired Justices Whittaker and Frankfurter. Among the issues receiving the most attention during the argument period were: the lack of other remedies in all the cases; the "consensus of lower courts" in moving toward representative equality; what "rational" deviations from population equality can be justified by a state; and the role of geography in the accessibility of a legislator to his constituents. In the discussions concerning equality of population, several Justices and counsel used as a rule of thumb the minimum percentage of the electorate that could control a legislative house. (See Chapter 3.) The very use of this index was a helpful sign for the plaintiffs, since the percentages, frequently low in any case, dramatize the impression of minority rule. The impact of *Gray v. Sanders* was also evident, since the "general principles of equality" the Court laid down in that case were reiterated by several of the attorneys for plaintiffs, doubtless convincing Justice Harlan that the fears he then expressed were far from groundless. During the many hours of close questioning from the bench, Harlan repeatedly pressed counsel about the intent and assumptions of the Fourteenth Amendment and whether the apportionment problem involved a proper application of its guarantee.

Filing briefs for the United States Government as a friend of the Court on behalf of the parties contesting state apportionment patterns was the Solicitor General, Archibald Cox. While urging the Court to find each of the state districting arrangements contrary to the Fourteenth Amendment's equal protection clause, Cox did not argue that there could never be any significant departure from population equality in either house of a state legislature. He added that there was no need for the high tribunal at that time to decide this ultimate question. According to the Solicitor General, the Fourteenth Amendment leaves room for accommodating "other permissible objectives" than simply per capita equality. Yet his argument went on to insist that population equality is the starting point and the fundamental standard, departures from which must serve a "valid governmental purpose." The burden is on the state to justify inequalities. Among permissible objectives could be the desire to represent communities or political subunits, so long as the result did not "submerge" the vital principles of voter equality and majority rule. But the mere protection of rural areas as such, for example, would be "class legislation" and not permissible. What Cox was basically arguing for was the general principle of representative equality but with some degree of flexibility to meet the needs of individual states. The Solicitor General went on to show how each of the cases on appeal failed to meet the criteria he urged.[23]

Presenting a different set of problems from the state cases were the challenges to congressional districts in Georgia and New York. In the former case the problem was a familiar one: great disparities (over 3 to 1) among the populations of outdated districts. But the New York case, involving districts whose populations were all within a reasonably close range, was more intricate. The question related to the way the lines were drawn in Manhattan. What had actually occurred was a partisan gerrymander by the Republican legislature, designed to retain for that party the seventeenth district, a "silk stocking" constituency centering on the upper-income areas of the East Side. As a result, the make-up of the district was 95 percent white, while nearly all of the borough's Negroes and Puerto Ricans were in Manhattan's other three districts, all safely Democratic. Complainants, largely Democratic county leaders, urged that the precedent in *Gomillion v. Lightfoot*, among others, forbade this kind of boundary drawing. But the Supreme Court decided that there was no proof that the motive was racial discrimination. Speaking for the majority, Justice Black pointed out that the concentration of racial and ethnic voters in particular areas of the borough strongly conditioned the type of districts that could be drawn.[24] Justices Douglas and Goldberg dissented in this case decided on February 17, 1964.

On the same day, the high tribunal announced its more important decision, *Wesberry v. Sanders*. This was the challenge to Georgia's failure to redraw congressional districts. In a 6 to 3 decision bound to create widespread revisions of districts throughout the nation, the Court declared that ". . . construed in its historical context, the command of Article I, Section 2, that Representatives be chosen 'by the People of the several States' means that as nearly as practicable one man's vote in a Congressional election is to be worth as much as another's." [25] Speaking for the majority, Justice Hugo Black added that it would defeat the principle of equal representation of people in the lower house of Congress if states could draw district lines in such a way as to give some voters a greater voice than others.

Justice Harlan (on the Court since 1955) began his impassioned oral dissent by noting: "I consider this occasion certainly the most solemn since I have been on this Court. And I think one would have to search the pages of history to find a case whose importance equals what we have decided today." [26] Harlan proceeded with an exhaustive survey of the historical background and language of Article I, Section 2, demonstrating clearly, he thought, that its purpose was only to deal with the apportionment of representatives *among* states, not to lay down a rule of equality *within* states. The dissenter stressed the inherent dangers of the decision to the principle of separation of powers. Moreover, "what is done today saps the political process. The promise of judicial intervention in matters of this sort cannot but encourage popular inertia in efforts for political reform through the political process . . ." [27]

Justice Stewart joined the dissent, although he rejected any implications that apportionment cases are not judiciable. Finally, Justice Clark concurred in part and dissented in part. He felt that Justice Harlan had much the better of the historical argument over the meaning of Article I; but he added that the case should be examined against the requirements of the equal protection clause of the Fourteenth Amendment, and he would have remanded it to the lower court for a hearing on the merits.

Why Justice Black specifically avoided basing the congressional districting decision on the Fourteenth Amendment's equal protection clause is puzzling, especially since he had stressed that ground in his earlier *Colegrove* dissent. By resting their argument on the logic and historical background of Article I, Section 2, Black and the Court's majority left themselves vulnerable to the penetrating and convincing rebuttal by Justice Harlan. The dissenter clearly demonstrated that the common assumption in the constitutional debates was that the section in question referred to the *apportionment* of congressional seats among states and not to the districting within them. Particularly damaging was Harlan's exhaustive documentation showing that the fourth section of Article I, giving Congress the power to alter state regulations of elections, was regarded as the remedy for state abuses of discretion in congressional districting.

The best that can be said for the Court's opinion in *Wesberry* is that equal districting is a logical corollary of the principle that representatives be chosen by the people. But, as Justice Clark suggested in his separate opinion, the Fourteenth Amendment's equal protection clause makes a more persuasive constitutional basis. Perhaps Justice Black and the Court majority wished to distinguish clearly between the problem of congressional districting and the question of the apportionment of state legislatures which was to be decided later in the term.

When the Supreme Court announced its anxiously awaited decisions on the latter question on June 15, 1964, the sweeping result and forthright language surprised many on both sides of the general controversy. The six states involved in these decisions represented a wide diversity of conditions which had been challenged: a state's failure to reapportion both houses in accordance with population standards indicated by its own constitution (Virginia); a state's use of complex population formulas in both houses to underrepresent the most populous counties (New York); apportionment provisos, ignoring population in both houses, frozen into the state constitution (Delaware); an upper house frozen into the state constitution, with a lower house apportioned partially in a population direction in the wake of *Baker v. Carr* (Maryland); a temporary reapportionment ordered by a Federal court, with state proposals for a "little federal" plan, neither house being based on population (Alabama); and, finally, a recently enacted constitutional amendment, sponsored by initiative petition and ratified by the state's voters, apportioning the lower house on population and the senate on a modified population base (Colorado). All of the challenged apportionments were declared invalid on federal constitutional grounds.

In spite of the fact that the six cases represented such an intricate variety of institutional arrangements and practices—or perhaps because of it—the Supreme Court expounded a general constitutional rule applicable to all of these cases, and, by plain implication, to all other state systems. The controlling philosophy is found in the Alabama case of *Reynolds v. Sims*. Speaking for the six-man majority, Chief Justice Warren declared:

> By holding that as a federal constitutional requisite both houses of a state legislature must be apportioned on a population basis, we mean that the Equal Protection Clause requires that a state make an honest and good faith effort to construct districts, in both houses of its legislature, as nearly of equal population as is practicable.[28]

The high tribunal added that mathematical exactness or precision was not required and declined to suggest any numerical or percentage guidelines. "What is marginally permissible in one state may be unsatisfactory in another, depending on the particular circumstances of the case," the opinion continued. The Chief Justice expressed confidence that lower courts could work out specific and appropriate standards in the context of actual litigation on a case-by-case basis.

Nonetheless, the supreme bench did state a few general considerations as guidelines for future cases. Some deviations from an equal population plan in either or both houses of a state legislature are constitutionally permissible "so long as the divergences from a strict equal population standard are based on legitimate considerations incident to the effectuation of a rational state policy." [29] Recognition of political subdivisions and community interests could be employed to some degree, but "population is, of necessity, the starting point for consideration and the controlling criterion for judgment in legislative apportionment controversies." [30]

Specifically disapproved was the federal analogy, the contention that states may base one of their legislative houses, as in the national Congress, on the equal representation of units of government rather than of people. The Court pointed to the fact that the original constitutions of nearly three-fourths of all the states provided for both houses based entirely or predominantly on population, suggesting that more recent support for the federal analogy is commonly an after-the-fact rationalization in defense of malapportionment. The accepted constitutional status of local units such as counties and towns within a unitary state, the Court pointed out, furnishes no parallel for a comparison with states in the federal union.

Unquestionably the most far-reaching of the six decisions announced on June 15, 1964, was the case of *Lucas v. The Forty-Fourth General Assembly of the State of Colorado*. In all the companion cases the lack of any realistic remedy to malapportionment posed a convincing case for judicial consideration. But the apportionment formula challenged in Colorado was itself the product of an initiative petition ratified in 1962 in all counties of the state, including Denver. Moreover, the new constitutional amendment established a lower house based on population and entailed comparatively modest deviations from population in the upper house. Finally, to make the case even sharper, the voters at the same election had rejected an alternative amendment which would have based both houses on population only. The Supreme Court majority frankly acknowledged most of these distinguishing characteristics.

The decision holding the Colorado plan unconstitutional suggests the key to the newly expressed judicial philosophy that the basic issue at stake in legislative apportionment is the right of the individual to cast an equally weighted vote. As for the fact that Colorado's voters had specifically chosen a less equal districting plan, Chief Justice Warren answered for the Court: "A citizen's constitutional rights can hardly be infringed simply because a majority of the people choose to do so." [31]

Dissenting in the decisions for all six states, Justice Harlan reiterated his view expressed in earlier cases that the judiciary was intruding dangerously and needlessly into the political process, and that the subject matter was not amenable to the development of judicial standards. A detailed analysis of the language, drafting, ratification, and subsequent history of the Fourteenth Amendment clearly demonstrated to Justice Harlan that the "Equal Protection Clause was never intended to inhibit the States in choosing any democratic method they pleased for the apportionment of their legislatures." [32]

A more complex position was argued by Justice Stewart (joined by Justice Clark), who asserted that the equal protection clause does restrict state legislative apportionments in two ways: they must be rational in the light of each state's own characteristics and needs; and they must not be so constructed as "systematically to prevent ultimate effective majority rule." But beyond these considerations, "there is nothing in the Federal

Constitution to prevent a State from choosing any electoral legislative structure it thinks best suited to the interests, temper, and customs of its people." [33] Applying these criteria, Stewart and Clark dissented from the rulings affecting Colorado and New York. They concurred with the results, but not the constitutional reasoning, in the remaining four cases.[34]

In some respects the Stewart-Clark approach to the question has considerable merit. The most serious malapportionments would be invalidated under their more limited yet positive application of the equal protection clause. Rationality and ultimate effective majority rule appear as persuasive standards for states to meet—yet flexible enough to allow for separate adjustment to differing local and regional conditions. The judicial role would at least *appear* more cautious and deliberate, though the power to determine what districting patterns meet the two general standards would inevitably involve the courts in difficult choices, a decision-making role which is hardly passive. And judges would surely differ in applying the standards, as Stewart and Clark themselves did concerning Ohio in the second set of state cases decided on June 22, 1964. Even their articulate dissent in the first set of cases announced a week earlier raises questions. Their dissent in the Colorado case is understandable enough. But for New York, a strong case could be made that one type of majority rule has long been kept from ultimate and effective expression. Justice Stewart's discussion of New York State ignores the party system and partisan geography, while computing arithmetical majorities from areas of highly dissimilar interests—a display of the same lack of political realism of which he accused the majority in its "one person, one vote" approach.

In any event, the decisions of June 15, along with the nine cases disposed of without opinion a week later, brought to fifteen the number of states whose legislative make-up was now deemed to violate the Fourteenth

Amendment's equal protection clause. Moreover, these decisions clearly presaged a similar fate for most of the state apportionments challenged and under consideration in lower courts, Federal or state. While the Supreme Court's majority opinion set no mathematical standards, it seemed clear that no more than a half dozen states could escape the task of redistricting. And while no time limit had been decreed, the supreme tribunal had indicated that no further legislative elections should ordinarily be held once an apportionment pattern is held unconstitutional. But it did suggest that the lower courts "reasonably" try "to avoid a disruption of the election process which might result from requiring precipitate changes that could make unreasonable or embarrassing demands on a State. . . ." [35]

Finally, the principle of one man, one vote, was soon extended to several local legislatures (county boards and city councils). Since most of these governing bodies are elected at large or are required by state law to represent districts of approximately equal population, only a small number of jurisdictions were directly affected by an application of recent Supreme Court decisions to local government. But this did occur in some states where laws or constitutions did not provide for equal representation at either city or county level. For example, in January, 1965, the Wisconsin Supreme Court unanimously ruled that the state's county boards must be elected on a population basis, concluding: "Since the composition of the legislature must conform to the principle of equal representation, it is logical that the arm or political subdivision of such legislature enacting legislation should be governed by the same principle of equal representation." [36]

The Political Counter-Revolution

Discussion and debate on these apportionment decisions was initially overshadowed by the congressional battle over the pending Civil Rights Act of 1964 and later by the activity surrounding the Republican National Convention. Yet the Republicans did include in their platform a plank revealing one type of reaction to the apportionment decisions—an effort to undercut the full effect of the Court's ruling by pledging "support of a Constitutional amendment . . . enabling states having bicameral legislatures to apportion one house on bases of their choosing, including factors other than population." [37] This plank made a paradoxical contrast with the earlier favorable reactions of the party's standard bearers for 1964, Senator Goldwater and Congressman Miller, to the Supreme Court's entry into the apportionment problem. As the campaign progressed, however, Senator Goldwater reversed that former position and criticized the Supreme Court for many of its opinions, including those on reapportionment. Democrats were sufficiently divided on this question that the party's 1964 platform remained silent on the apportionment controversy.

By August, 1964 congressional opposition to the new judicial interpretations had taken several forms. First came a move to amend the United States Constitution in the manner proposed by the Republican platform. But a second tactic, based on the limited time available for attempting to implement such an amendment, was a drive to withdraw the jurisdiction of Federal courts over either pending or future cases involving state legislative apportionment. A bill embodying these provisions was introduced in the House of Representatives by Congressman William Tuck of Virginia. In a highly unusual maneuver, the House Rules Committee cleared the bill for floor action without the consideration of the Judiciary Committee, chaired by Congressman Emanuel Celler of New York, an opponent of the Tuck measure. On August 19, the House passed the bill by a vote of 218 to 175, with most support coming from Republicans and Southern Democrats. So drastic a statute had not been passed since Congress denied the Supreme Court appellate jurisdiction over the Reconstruction Acts after the Civil War.

Still another approach materialized in the Senate: an attempt to secure time for later consideration of a constitutional amendment by withdrawing apportionment cases from the jurisdiction of Federal courts for a period of two to four years. Originally proposed by the minority leader, Everett Dirksen, as a rider to the foreign aid bill, the measure was later modified by an agreement with the Senate Democratic leadership and the Justice Department so as to authorize temporary stays of court apportionment orders, in the absence of "highly unusual circumstances." [38] The intervention of the Justice Department was apparently caused by the desire to moderate the proposal in an acceptable direction, since chances of its passage were regarded as good. But Senate liberals launched a "baby" filibuster which ended the leadership's hopes for congressional adjournment prior to the Democratic National Convention. The debate, both before and after the convention, appeared to build strength for the liberal opposition, whose filibuster easily survived an attempt at cloture on September 10 by a vote of 30 to 63. The Senate eventually passed a mild "sense of Congress" amendment which urged, rather than ordered, lower Federal courts to give state legislatures up to six months to comply with reapportionment decrees. Passage was considered a victory for the Court's supporters, since the measure was opposed largely by senators favorable to the original Dirksen rider. Indeed, due to this switch of positions, the bill failed of passage in the House, where proponents of strong curbs on the Federal courts considered the Senate-passed measure worse than taking no action at all. Since the House-passed Tuck bill had never had a chance of Senate passage, the result of over a month of heated congressional debate was no official position by the national lawmakers prior to adjournment.

This negative outcome did not end the hopes of those

attempting to reverse or modify the judicial revolution. Efforts to amend the United States Constitution were resumed with fresh vigor in Congress, with sponsors encouraged by the fact that some opposition to the Dirksen rider had been motivated not so much by a defense of legislative reapportionment as by a wish to avoid rebuking the Supreme Court. The lead was again taken by Senator Dirksen, who introduced a constitutional amendment which would allow states to apportion one house of a bicameral legislature on the basis of factors other than population, if approved by popular referendum. In an attempt to gain more support, a provision for future state referenda after each census was added. When the proposed amendment was blocked in the Senate Judiciary Committee by a tie vote, Senator Dirksen brought it to the floor as a substitute for a pending resolution. Most opposition came from a group of liberal Democrats, led by Senators Paul Douglas of Illinois and Joseph Tydings of Maryland, who concluded that a filibuster was unnecessary this time. On August 4, 1965, the Senate divided 57 in favor to 39 against the proposal, seven votes short of the necessary two-thirds.

A key factor in the defeat of the Dirksen amendment appeared to be the argument that it would allow state legislatures to dilute Negro voting strength through the use of nonpopulation factors in one house. In the South, suffrage among Negroes has been far more widespread in urban than in rural areas. During the summer of 1965 the Leadership Conference on Civil Rights (representing nearly 100 civil rights organizations) assumed a leading role in the campaign on Capitol Hill against all proposed amendments which would modify the apportionment rulings.

Finally, the campaign to sponsor a constitutional amendment via a petition of three-fourths of the state legislatures, apparently stilled since the summer of 1963, revived by 1965. By July 2 of that year, a total of twenty-seven legislatures had passed such a proposal.[39]

Yet time appeared now to be on the side of those defending the Supreme Court's reapportionment rulings, with the continued restructuring of state legislatures by judicial prodding.

Problems and Prospects

The apportionment decisions of 1964 reveal a profound judicial reassessment of the relationship between citizens and their state governments. The traditional viewpoint had been that legislative apportionment is a problem of government structure, deeply intertwined with politics, and that courts should not interfere with the prerogatives of the states regarding their own institutions (or of a co-equal branch in the case of congressional districts). In contrast, the new interpretation, formulated and expressed by the Supreme Court's majority, begins at a different point in the political process: the individual. Representative equality is regarded as an aspect of voting rights, as necessary of judicial protection as other guarantees of equality.

The concept of equal representation as an individual right is not in itself new. It found frequent expression in America in the eighteenth and nineteenth centuries, as we have seen in Chapter 2. It is unquestionably true, as Justices Frankfurter and Harlan insisted, that such ideas were not assumed to be embodied in federal constitutional provisos. But to demonstrate that is not enough. Constitutional interpretation has not been restricted to the literal language or intent of the major provisions. The adaptability of the Constitution to the monumental changes which have characterized American society and institutions is due in part to judicial recognition of the nagging political issues confronting each age. In view of the relative lack of nonjudicial solutions, the central question in the apportionment controversy was whether there was a legal remedy for a widespread and growing institutional inequality. As

Walter Lippmann reflected after the June, 1964 decisions, "Without the intervention of the court to push the states off dead center, the American political system may become paralyzed." [40]

In addition to its immediate and visible impact on legislative institutions, the vigorous entry of judicial power into the matter of apportionment has served a more subtle, yet promising, function. This is the potential re-examination of the whole concept of representative government in a complex modern society. "It should open the way at last," in the words of Professor Robert G. Dixon, Jr., "to a fresh dialogue—long overdue—about the character and function of representation in a Twentieth Century mass democracy." [41] Professor Dixon perceptively points out that the Supreme Court's emphasis on representative equality as an individual right obscures the crucial fact that the personal civil right of the voter is necessarily intertwined with group activity in the process of representation. These relationships need a new exploration which was not undertaken while the debate on representation was necessarily conditioned by the struggle over population equality.

Moreover, the principle of one person, one vote, is at best a starting point. Chief Justice Warren articulated the Supreme Court's philosophy that "fair and effective representation for all citizens is concededly the basic aim of legislative apportionment." [42] Attempts to maximize this goal may require more than accepting a districting pattern which is substantially equal. While the Court has understandably appeared reluctant to scrutinize partisan gerrymanders, these furnish one example of how "fair representation" can be vitiated even under the equal population principle. Furthermore, such matters as single-member versus multimember districts raise intriguing questions as to the nature of representative government. Thus the widespread use of multimember districts in several urban areas, especially in the South, poses numerous problems, including the underrepresentation of the minority party (or other minority groupings, including racial). This issue arose in 1962 when the state of Georgia passed a constitutional amendment allowing at-large elections for counties with more than one senator, a move widely regarded as a means of preventing the election of a Negro senator from Atlanta. The next year the Federal district court held that the Georgia legislature's creation of both single-member and multimember districts was a form of invidious discrimination. On appeal, the Supreme Court in January, 1965 overruled the lower tribunal, noting that its recent decision in the Alabama case (*Reynolds v. Sims*) had specifically allowed such an arrangement.[43] Nevertheless, the make-up of constituencies will increasingly demand the attention of those concerned with the elusive goal of "fair and effective representation of all citizens." It is even possible that some interest will focus on certain forms of proportional representation as a means of minimizing the problems of gerrymandering as well as the hazards of at-large elections.

One point seems clear. The frequently expressed charge that the Supreme Court has imposed a uniform pattern on all the states is far from the truth. Indeed, for all their diversities, the state apportionment patterns existing prior to judicial activism betrayed a general lack of imagination or experimentation with new representative forms. In many ways, the Court has encouraged or necessitated a sober reconsideration of a variety of forms in creating constituencies and electing representatives. The confusion created in some states by the haste imposed by overzealous lower courts has perhaps obscured this point. But initial reallocation of political power, whether accomplished quickly under duress or more deliberately, need not preclude further refinements and the consideration of alternative ways of providing effective and meaningful representation to all important segments composing the broader political community. A period of institutional remodeling offers considerable opportunity to bring creative and constructive ideas to bear on one of the central questions facing modern American democracy.

NOTES TO THE STUDY

CHAPTER 1—Years of Decisions: 1962–1964

1. *Reynolds v. Sims*, 377 U.S. 567 (1964).
2. *WMCA v. Lomenzo*, 377 U.S. 748 (1964).
3. Extemporaneous remarks as reported by Anthony Lewis, *The New York Times*, June 16, 1964.
4. *Reynolds v. Sims*, 377 U.S. 624–625 (1964).
5. 369 U.S. 186 (1962).
6. Quoted in *The New York Times*, March 28, 1962.
7. *Public Papers of the Presidents: John F. Kennedy, 1962* (Washington: U.S. Government Printing Office, 1963), p. 274.
8. Quoted in *The New York Times*, March 28, 1962.
9. AP dispatch, *Santa Barbara News-Press*, March 28, 1962.
10. Quoted in *The New York Times*, March 28, 1962.
11. "An End to Government by Minority: The Reapportionment Results of *Baker v. Carr*," address before joint meeting of American Political Science Association and the National Municipal League, September 8, 1962, Washington, D.C. (mimeographed), pp. 1, 4.
12. Data in this paragraph are based on Paul T. David and Ralph Eisenberg, *State Legislative Redistricting: Major Issues in the Wake of Judicial Decision* (Chicago: Public Administration Service, 1962), pp. 2–5; and *National Civic Review* (section on Representation) for October, November, and December, 1962.
13. *Congressional Quarterly Weekly Report*, XXI (March 22, 1963), 424.
14. *Ibid.*
15. *Wesberry v. Sanders*, 376 U.S. 1 at 7–8 (1964).
16. *Wright v. Rockefeller*, 376 U.S. 52 (1964).
17. Both quotations from *The New York Times*, June 17, 1964.

CHAPTER 2—Representative Equality in American Thought and Practice

1. Judge Simeon S. Willis in *Stiglitz v. Schardien*, 239 Ky. at 812 (1931).
2. Emily Allyn, "Rotten Boroughs," *Encyclopedia of Social Sciences* (New York: The Macmillan Company, 1934), XIII, 443–44.
3. Robert Luce, *Legislative Principles* (Boston: Houghton Mifflin Company, 1930), p. 338.
4. *The Writings of Thomas Jefferson*, Library Edition (Washington, 1903), Vol. II, 160–61.

5. Quoted in Luce, *op. cit.*, p. 344.

6. Max Farrand (ed.), *The Records of the Federal Convention of 1787* (New Haven: Yale University Press, 1911), Vol. I, 185.

7. *Ibid.*, p. 562.

8. *The Federalist*, No. 62.

9. See Elisha P. Douglass, *Rebels and Democrats: The Struggle for Equal Political Rights and Majority Rule During the American Revolution* (Chapel Hill: The University of North Carolina Press, 1955).

10. I Stat. 50–2 (1787): *An Act to Provide for the Government of the Territory Northwest of the River Ohio.*

11. Advisory Commission on Intergovernmental Relations, *Apportionment of State Legislatures* (Washington: U.S. Government Printing Office, December, 1962), p. 10. This source has a useful table indicating a breakdown by categories and chronological periods of the types of apportionment provisos found in original state constitutions.

Robert G. Dixon, Jr., has arrived at a smaller number of such states in his analysis found in "Reapportionment in the Supreme Court and Congress: Constitutional Struggle for Fair Representation," *Michigan Law Review*, LXIII (December, 1964), 239–242. The discrepancy is apparently the result of different interpretations as to when a state constitution provided an apportionment basis *predominantly* on population.

12. A good example of this point can be seen in the data disclosed by Ernest C. Reock, Jr., in *Population Inequality Among Counties in the New Jersey Legislature, 1791–1962* (New Brunswick: Bureau of Government Research, Rutgers, The State University, 1963), especially pp. 21–22. Reock shows that even such a highly unequal standard as New Jersey's one senator per county rule did not produce a critical representative imbalance during the early part of the nineteenth century when the state's population was spread quite uniformly.

13. Quoted in Luce, *op. cit.*, pp. 346–47.

Chapter 3—Representation at the State Level

1. "The national averages are in many ways an understatement of the situations to which they relate. In any system of averages, the ends of the range become blurred. . . . Finally, the use of fixed categories of counties by size, although necessary for statistical analysis and comparison, has a built-in tendency to slow down the divergence of the averages as counties grow in population and shift up from one category to another." Paul T. David and Ralph Eisenberg, *Devaluation of the Urban and Suburban Vote* (Charlottesville, Va.: Bureau of Public Administration, University of Virginia, 1961), Vol. I, 10.

2. Much of the material in this paragraph is based on Thomas Page, *Legislative Apportionment in Kansas* (Lawrence, Kan.: Bureau of Government Research, University of Kansas, 1952).

3. Karl A. Bosworth, "Law Making in State Governments," in *The Forty-Eight States: Their Tasks as Policy Makers and Administrators* (New York: The American Assembly, Graduate School of Business, Columbia University, 1955), p. 95.

4. For a good discussion of this question, see Robert McKay, *Reapportionment and The Federal Analogy* (New York: The National Municipal League, 1962).

5. *One Man, One Vote* (New York: The Twentieth Century Fund, 1962).

6. Manning J. Dauer and Robert G. Kelsay, "Unrepresentative States," *National Municipal Review*, XLIV (December, 1955), 571–575. Statistical corrections in issue of April, 1956. The actual percentages are affected to some degree by the size of the house. In most cases a majority of the legislature could not be elected by a majority of voters even if the least populous districts were within a fairly close range of the norm; but any percentage from 45 to 50 can be regarded as highly representative in terms of population.

7. See Introduction by William J. D. Boyd to 1962 edition of *Compendium on Legislative Apportionment* (New York: The National Municipal League, 1962).

8. For a much more complicated method of computing a comparative index for all states, see Glendon Schubert and Charles Press, "Measuring Malapportionment," *American Political Science Review*, LVIII (June, 1964), 302–327. (See communications and corrected data in the December, 1964 issue of the same *Review*, 966–970.) While this is a sophisticated and imaginative analysis of the many factors which comprise malapportionment, it also weighs these factors in a somewhat arbitrary manner. Many (probably most) of the close students of legislative apportionment would quarrel with the authors' scale, which concludes that Ohio was the best apportioned state and Minnesota next to last in 1962. For another look at this problem, see Alan L. Clem, "Measuring Legislative Malapportionment: In Search of a Better Yardstick," *Midwest Journal of Political Science*, VII (May, 1963), 125–144.

9. The reasons for the equalization in these three states are not hard to discover. The constitutions of Oregon and Alaska have well-designed reapportionment enforcement provisions, with the safeguard of judicial scrutiny if needed; Minnesota's figures represent the impact of a judicially prodded redistricting in 1959 (discussed in Chapter 7).

10. See V. O. Key, Jr., *Southern Politics* (New York: Alfred A. Knopf, 1949), especially pp. 5–6, 43.

11. Malcolm E. Jewell, *The State Legislature: Politics and Practice* (New York: Random House, 1962), pp. 30–31.

12. *Ibid.*, pp. 31–32.

13. *Gray v. Sanders,* 372 U.S. 368 (1963).

14. William C. Havard and Loren P. Beth, *The Politics of Misrepresentation: Rural-Urban Conflict in the Florida Legislature* (Baton Rouge, La.: Louisiana State University Press, 1962), p. 217.

15. List of campaign contributors as reported in *Santa Barbara News-Press,* December 7, 1962.

16. Charles C. Killingsworth, *State Labor Relations Acts* (Chicago: University of Chicago Press, 1948), p. 20.

17. For varying responses on the effects of the apportionment pattern in all the states, see the state-by-state opinions compiled in the National Municipal League's *Compendium on Legislative Apportionment, op. cit.* The appraisals on the matter of effects differ substantially in their completeness, and many of the correspondents apparently did not understand the meaning of the question. For these reasons such interpretive material in the *Compendium* must be regarded as suggestive rather than diagnostic; certainly it seems pointless to attempt to draw quantitative conclusions from them as Alfred de Grazia did in his *Apportionment and Representative Government* (New York: Praeger, 1963), pp. 102–107. The only meaningful way to understand the effects of apportionment is through close analyses of particular states; the nearest approximation of this is probably Havard and Beth's work on Florida (note 14), though this state is admittedly an extreme case and would hardly be considered "typical."

18. Havard and Beth, *op. cit.*, p. 77.

19. "The Eighth American Assembly Participants' Findings," *The Forty-Eight States: Their Tasks as Policy Makers and Administrators, op. cit.*, p. 139. The participants in this meeting of the Assembly consisted of fifty-five leaders from all parts of the country drawn from business, labor, agriculture, the professions, education, local, state and national governments.

Chapter 4—Metropolitan America: New Dimension of Rural-Urban Conflict

1. A. Whitney Griswold, *Democracy and Farming* (New Haven: Yale University Press, 1952), p. 137.

2. Lane Lancaster, *Government in Rural America,* 2nd ed. (Princeton, N.J.: D. Van Nostrand Company, Inc., 1952), pp. 57–58.

3. Joseph Allan Beek, *The California Legislature* (Sacramento: California State Printing Office, 1957), p. 8.

4. Charles R. Adrian, *Governing Urban America,* 2nd ed. (New York: McGraw-Hill Book Company, Inc., 1961), p. 46.

5. Victor Jones, "American Local Government in a Changing Federalism," reprint from the *American Review,* II (May, 1962),

3, published by the University of California Institute of Governmental Studies, Berkeley.

6. *Ibid.*, pp. 8–9.

7. *Ibid.*, p. 9.

8. David W. Minar and Scott Greer, "The Metropolis and Its Problems," *1963–1964 American Government Annual* (New York: Holt, Rinehart, and Winston Company, 1963), p. 114.

9. *Ibid.*

10. Paul T. David and Ralph Eisenberg, *Devaluation of the Urban and Suburban Vote* (Charlottesville, Va.: Bureau of Public Administration, University of Virginia, 1961), Vol. I, 12–13. One problem posed by the David-Eisenberg method of using statistical data on a county basis is seen in the figures for the Chicago area. A 1954 apportionment increased suburban Cook County's share of senate strength from one to six and also rearranged city districts. Yet the figure for Cook County cannot reveal the relationship of city and suburbs in the representative pattern.

11. Conclusions in this paragraph are based partially upon an extensive survey reported in Gordon E. Baker, "Cities Resent Stepchild Lot," *National Municipal Review*, XLII (September, 1953), 387–92. For attitudes of the United States Conference of Mayors, with supporting data, see especially two brochures published by that organization in 1948: *Government of the People, by the People, for the People;* and *Representation is the Basis of Our Structure of Government.*

12. Hugh Douglas Price, "Florida: Politics and the 'Pork Choppers,'" in Malcolm E. Jewell, ed., *The Politics of Reapportionment* (New York: Atherton Press, 1962), p. 89.

13. For a detailed, if dated, account of a political battle between New York City and the state over fiscal matters in 1954, see the case study in Gordon E. Baker, *Rural Versus Urban Political Power* (New York: Random House, 1955), pp. 32–39. While this particular situation is now history, similar frictions have occurred periodically since the episode cited.

14. Edward O. Banfield and James Q. Wilson, *City Politics* (Cambridge, Mass.: Harvard University Press and Massachusetts Institute of Technology Press, 1963), p. 68.

15. *Ibid.*, p. 71.

16. David R. Derge has revealed the lack of cohesion among metropolitan legislators on roll call votes in two states in his article, "Metropolitan and Outstate Alignments in Illinois and Missouri Legislative Delegations," *American Political Science Review*, LII (December, 1958), 1051–65. However, Derge proceeds to draw more conclusions than seem warranted by his data. See Richard Frost's rejoinder in the same journal, LIII (September, 1959), 792–95.

17. Commission on Intergovernmental Relations, *A Report to*

the President for Transmittal to the Congress (Washington: U.S. Government Printing Office, 1955), p. 40.

18. Robert S. Friedman, "The Urban-Rural Conflict Revisited," *Western Political Quarterly*, XIV (June, 1961), 485.

19. Commission on Intergovernmental Relations, *op. cit.*, p. 39.

Chapter 5–Representation at the National Level

The author acknowledges the assistance of Mr. Thomas V. Martin in helping to gather and compute much of the data for this chapter.

1. As recently as 1952, Professor Alfred de Grazia perpetuated the notion: "The United States Senate, which was not created to represent the country areas, has become a stronghold of rural representation." A. de Grazia, *Public and Republic* (New York: Alfred A. Knopf, 1951), p. 169.

2. Quoted in Joel Paschal, "The House of Representatives: 'Grand Depository of the Democratic Principle'?" *Law and Contemporary Problems*, XVII (Spring, 1952), 276–89.

3. Quoted in *ibid.*, p. 278.

4. See *Congressional Quarterly Weekly Report* (March 19, 1965), pp. 419–420. For the earlier recommendations of the American Political Science Association, see "The Reapportionment of Congress," *The American Political Science Review*, XLV (March, 1951), 153–57.

5. Compare the tables in this chapter with those in Gordon E. Baker, *Rural Versus Urban Political Power* (New York: Random House, 1955), pp. 43–44.

6. Andrew Hacker, *Congressional Districting: The Issue of Equal Representation* (Washington: The Brookings Institution, 1963), pp. 97–98.

7. See *ibid.*, pp. 94–101, for Hacker's interesting statistical work on average district deviations.

8. *Congressional Quarterly Weekly Report* (February 2, 1962), p. 153.

9. See Hacker, *op. cit.*, pp. 86–87, for a still different four-category breakdown of districts devised by Hacker; under his criteria, there was a surplus of sixteen rural seats and a deficiency of ten and six respectively by suburban and mid-urban groupings.

10. *Congressional Quarterly Weekly Report* (March 19, 1965), p. 419.

11. For a summary of the various areas affected by the 1961 gerrymander in New York, see Gus Tyler and David Wells, "New York: Constitutionally Republican," in Malcolm E. Jewell, *The Politics of Reapportionment* (New York: Atherton Press, 1962), esp. pp. 224–30.

12. Figures adapted from H. Frank Way, "California: 'Brutal Butchery of the Two-Party System'?" in *ibid.*, p. 260.

13. See Robert A. Dahl, *A Preface to Democratic Theory* (Chicago: University of Chicago Press, 1956), p. 146; and Hacker, *op. cit.*, pp. 43–46.

14. Republicans lost one of their eight by a scant margin in the Democratic landslide of 1958, but regained that district in 1960, when they lost a different district. Thus, the total of the GOP in Los Angeles county never fell below seven.

15. Hacker, *op. cit.*, p. 57. Hacker's third chapter contains an excellent discussion of gerrymandering, with some interesting statistical data and case studies in the three key states of New York, California, and Michigan.

16. *Ibid.*

17. Quoted in *Congressional Quarterly*, X (May, 1952), 463.

18. Quoted in *The New York Times*, December 6, 1951, p. 26.

19. *Wright v. Rockefeller*, 376 U.S. 52 (1964).

20. *Congressional Quarterly Weekly Report*, XIV (March 30, 1956), 364.

21. Peter H. Odegard, *Pressure Politics: The Story of the Anti-Saloon League* (New York: Columbia University Press, 1928), p. 121.

22. Cyril F. Brickfield, "State Applications Asking Congress to Call a Federal Constitutional Convention," 87th Cong., 1st sess., 1961 (printed by the Committee on the Judiciary).

23. Charles L. Black, Jr., "The Proposed Amendment of Article V: A Threatened Disaster," *Yale Law Journal*, LXXII (April, 1963), 957–66.

CHAPTER 6—One Man, One Vote: A Critique

1. Commission on Intergovernmental Relations, *A Report to the President for Transmittal to the Congress* (Washington: U.S. Government Printing Office, 1955), p. 40.

2. Advisory Commission on Intergovernmental Relations, *Apportionment of State Legislatures* (Washington: U.S. Government Printing Office, December, 1962), p. 77.

3. *Reynolds v. Sims* (Alabama case), 377 U.S. 578–579 (1964).

4. *Ibid.*

5. See dissent by Justice William O. Douglas in *South v. Peters* 339 U.S. 276 at 278 (1950).

6. *Reynolds v. Sims*, 377 U.S. 566. For a perceptive analysis of the majority-minority dichotomy, see Robert A. Dahl, *A Preface to Democratic Theory* (Chicago: University of Chicago Press, 1956), especially Chapter 5.

Chapter 7—The Judicial Revolution

Thanks to a travel grant from the Committee on Research of the University of California, Santa Barbara, the author was able to witness oral argument before the Supreme Court in November, 1963. Commentary in the text on this phase of the judicial consideration is drawn from that observation.

1. While constitutional conventions are relatively rare, Michigan did hold one in 1961–1962, which drafted a new constitution. For studies of the convention and the crucial political role played by the apportionment issues, see Albert Sturm, *Constitution Making in Michigan, 1961–1962* (Ann Arbor, Mich.: Institute of Public Administration, University of Michigan, 1963); and Karl A. Lamb, "The Political Evolution of the Michigan Apportionment Formula," in Karl A. Lamb, William J. Pierce, and John P. White, *Apportionment and Representative Institutions: The Michigan Experience* (Washington: The Institute for Social Science Research, 1963).

2. See Gordon E. Baker, *The Politics of Reapportionment in Washington State*, Eagleton Institute Case Studies in Practical Politics (New York: McGraw-Hill, 1961); also "Reapportionment by Initiative in Oregon," *The Western Political Quarterly*, XIII (June, 1960), 508–19.

3. See Gordon E. Baker, "The California Senate: Sectional Conflict and *Vox Populi*," in Malcolm E. Jewell, *The Politics of Reapportionment* (New York: Atherton Press, 1962), pp. 51–63.

4. See Gordon E. Baker, "Legislative Power to Amend Initiatives in Washington State," *Pacific Northwest Quarterly*, LV (January, 1964), 28–35. A brief summary of applicable provisions in other states is included.

5. Alexis de Tocqueville, *Democracy in America* (New York: Alfred A. Knopf, Vintage Books, 1954), Vol. I, 290.

6. *Fergus v. Kinney*, 333 Ill. 437 (1928).

7. See Stanley Friedelbaum, "*Baker v. Carr:* The New Doctrine of Judicial Intervention and its Implications for American Federalism," *University of Chicago Law Review*, XXIX (Summer, 1962), 673–704.

8. *Colegrove v. Green*, 328 U.S. 549 at 556 (1946).

9. *Ibid.*, at 553–554.

10. *Ibid.*, at 556.

11. *Ibid.*, at 573.

12. For a more detailed discussion of developments underlying the shift in judicial outlook, see Gordon E. Baker, "Representative Equality: 'Political Thicket' or Voting Right?" in Gottfried Dietze (ed.), *Essays on the American Constitution* (Englewood Cliffs, N.J.: Prentice-Hall, 1964), pp. 23–42.

13. *Dyer v. Kazuhisa Abe*, 138F. Supp. 220 at 236.
14. *Magraw v. Donovan*, 163F. Supp. 187 (1958).
15. For a delightful account of this case, see Bernard Taper, *Gomillion v. Lightfoot* (New York: McGraw-Hill, 1962).
16. *Gomillion v. Lightfoot*, 364 U.S. 347 (1960).
17. *Baker v. Carr*, 179F. Supp. 826 (1959).
18. *Baker v. Carr*, 369 U.S. 267 (1962).
19. *Ibid.*, p. 270.
20. Alpheus T. Mason, *The Supreme Court from Taft to Warren* (Baton Rouge: Louisiana State University Press, 1958), p. 178.
21. *Gray v. Sanders*, 372 U.S. 379 (1963).
22. *Ibid.*, p. 381.
23. The Solicitor General's general argument appears in his brief for the Maryland case (*Maryland Committee for Fair Representation v. Tawes*). See esp. pp. 25–29 and 45–50. A useful summary of the argument is also found in the account by Anthony Lewis in *The New York Times*, November 14, 1963, p. 29.
24. *Wright v. Rockefeller*, 376 U.S. 52 (1964).
25. *Wesberry v. Sanders*, 376 U.S. 7–8.
26. As reported in *The New York Times*, February 18, 1964, p. 1.
27. *Wesberry v. Sanders*, 376 U.S. 48.
28. *Reynolds v. Sims*, 377 U.S. 577.
29. *Ibid.*, p. 579.
30. *Ibid.*, p. 567.
31. *Lucas v. The Forty-Fourth General Assembly of the State of Colorado*, 377 U.S. 736–737.
32. 377 U.S. 590–591.
33. 377 U.S. 754.
34. With this minor exception: Justice Stewart abstained in the Maryland case and would have remanded it for further hearings on the criterion of "ultimate effective majority rule."
35. 377 U.S. 585.
36. Quoted in *National Civic Review*, LIV (February, 1965), 96. For decisions affecting local governments in several states, see Volume XIII (New York: 1965) in the National Municipal League's series of published court decisions on legislative apportionment.
37. Quoted in *Santa Barbara News-Press*, July 16, 1964.
38. Cited in Congressional Quarterly's *CQ Guide to Current American Government*, Fall, 1964 (Washington, 1964), p. 54. This publication includes an excellent and detailed summary of congressional developments (see pp. 53–57).
39. *Congressional Quarterly Weekly Report*, XXIII (July 16, 1965), 1383.
40. *Santa Barbara News-Press*, June 18, 1964.
41. Robert G. Dixon, Jr., "Recent Developments in Reappor-

tionment: The Constitutional Struggle for Fair Representation," (mimeo. address to Conference of Chief Justices, August 6, 1964), p. 13.

42. *Reynolds v. Sims,* 377 U.S. 565–566.

43. *Fortson v. Dorsey,* 379 U.S. 433 (1965).

BIBLIOGRAPHIC NOTE

Since the notes for each chapter of this study have cited copious references to materials on legislative representation and apportionment, this section can be brief. Its aim is to alert the reader to some of the most recently published materials covering various aspects of the subject.

For the national level, dealing with the House of Representatives, the best single volume is Andrew Hacker's *Congressional Districting: The Issue of Equal Representation* (Washington: The Brookings Institution, 1963, 2nd ed., 1964). For the past several years, the Congressional Quarterly, Inc., has published invaluable materials, including studies of individual states, in its *Congressional Quarterly Weekly Report,* as well as periodic special reports on the nature and make-up of congressional constituencies. Maps, population figures, urban-rural and party ratios, and other useful data are included.

For state legislatures, the most comprehensive statistical data on the development of representative imbalances were published in Paul David and Ralph Eisenberg's *Devaluation of the Urban and Suburban Vote,* 2 vols. (Charlottesville, Va.: University of Virginia Bureau of Public Administration, 1961, 1962). Volume I is devoted to a general survey of comparative values of representative strength in state legislatures by categories of countries, both nationally and on a state-by-state basis, while Volume II consists of valuation figures for each state and its internal shifts for all counties from 1910 through 1960.

The National Municipal League has published a number of studies on the question of state legislative apportionment. Particularly since 1962, the League, assisted by foundation support, has become a major clearing house for materials on the subject. The mounting volume of judicial opinions of state and Federal courts on legislative apportionment has been reproduced by photo-offset in numerous volumes (totaling 15 by mid-1965). The League's periodical, *The National Civic Review,* published monthly (except August), contains frequent articles as well as a section on representation, which keeps track of new political and judicial developments in all the states. The *Review,* while displaying a bias toward a population standard for legislative districts, publishes articles from a variety of perspectives, including some at variance with the one person, one vote doctrine. A concise recap of apportionment practices in the light of recent judicial decisions is the League's pamphlet by William J. D. Boyd, entitled *Changing Patterns of Apportionment* (1965). Finally, Boyd and Ruth C. Silva compiled an extensive *Bibliography on Apportionment* (1963) published by the League and containing over 700 titles.

The political aspects of apportionment, largely neglected by scholars until recent years, form the focus of useful case studies of several states, edited by Malcolm E. Jewell, under the title *The Politics of Reapportionment* (New York: Atherton Press, 1962). Jewell's introductory essay is a valuable synthesis of the major features delineated by the other authors. Another case study of a single state's apportionment problem and its pervasive impact on the whole spectrum of political processes and institutions is Gordon E. Baker's *The Politics of Reapportionment in Washington State*, Eagleton Institute Case Studies in Practical Politics (New York: McGraw-Hill, 1960, 1961).

Judicial involvement in apportionment has precipitated a veritable floodtide of commentary, especially in law journals. An earlier survey of judicial practices, with a brief for a more active role for Federal courts, is Anthony Lewis' "Legislative Apportionment and the Federal Courts," *Harvard Law Review*, LXXI (April, 1958), 1057–1098. As a writer for *The New York Times*, Lewis also provided excellent coverage of the Supreme Court's apportionment decisions in the period 1962–1964. Of the numerous commentaries in the wake of *Baker v. Carr*, see the variety of approaches comprising the *Yale Law Journal's* special supplement, *The Problem of Malapportionment: A Symposium on Baker v. Carr*, LXXII (November, 1962). The same journal carried a lengthy and useful unsigned note, "*Baker v. Carr* and Legislative Apportionments: A Problem of Standards," LXXII (April, 1963), 968–1040. An issue of *Law and Contemporary Problems*, XXVII (Summer, 1962, Part II) devoted to "The Electoral Process" contains useful articles on judicial aspects of reapportionment by Ruth C. Silva, Robert G. Dixon, Jr., and Gus Tyler. A valuable critique summarizing the major cases and issues arising for decisions on the merits is Robert B. McKay's "Political Thickets and Crazy Quilts: Reapportionment and Equal Protection," *Michigan Law Review*, LXI (February, 1963), 645–710. The 1964 decisions produced still more analyses; in particular, see the excellent symposia in *The Notre Dame Lawyer*, XXXIX (1964) and *Michigan Law Review*, LXIII (December, 1964). Valuable both for its depth and its breadth is Carl A. Auerbach, "The Reapportionment Cases: One Person, One Vote —One Vote, One Value," *1964, The Supreme Court Review* (Chicago: The University of Chicago Press, 1965), pp. 1–87. An incisive and thoughtful summary and evaluation of the apportionment decisions is C. Herman Pritchett's 1964 presidential address before the American Political Science Association, "Equal Protection and the Urban Majority," *American Political Science*

Review, LVIII (December, 1964), 869–875. Finally, a concise, nontechnical summation of what the Supreme Court did and did not decide in its apportionment rulings of 1962–1964 is William J. D. Boyd's "Apportionment Facts," *National Civic Review*, LIII (November, 1964), 530–534, 544.

A brief anthology of commentary and judicial opinions is *Legislative Apportionment: Key to Power*, edited by Howard D. Hamilton (New York: Harper & Row, 1964). A much more complete collection of a variety of materials is the judiciously edited volume by Glendon Schubert, entitled *Reapportionment* (New York: Charles Scribner's Research Anthology, 1965).

APPENDIX

Baker v. Carr (369 U.S. 186) Decided March 26, 1962

MR. JUSTICE BRENNAN *delivered the opinion of the Court.*

This civil action was brought under 42 U.S.C. § 1983 and 1988 to redress the alleged deprivation of federal constitutional rights. The complaint, alleging that by means of a 1901 statute of Tennessee apportioning the members of the General Assembly among the State's 95 counties, "these plaintiffs and others similarly situated, are denied the equal protection of the laws accorded them by the Fourteenth Amendment to the Constitution of the United States by virtue of the debasement of their votes," was dismissed by a three-judge court convened under 28 U.S.C. § 2281 in the Middle District of Tennessee. The court held that it lacked jurisdiction of the subject matter and also that no claim was stated upon which relief could be granted. 179 F. Supp. 824. We noted probable jurisdiction of the appeal. 364 U.S. 898. We hold that the dismissal was error, and remand the cause to the District Court for trial and further proceedings consistent with this opinion. . . .

In light of the District Court's treatment of the case, we hold today only (a) that the court possessed jurisdiction of the subject matter; (b) that a justiciable cause of action is stated upon which appellants would be entitled to appropriate relief; and (c) because appellees raise the issue before this Court, that the appellants have standing to challenge the Tennessee apportionment statutes. Beyond noting that we have no cause at this stage to doubt the District Court will be able to fashion relief if violations of constitutional rights are found, it is improper now to consider what remedy would be most appropriate if appellants prevail at the trial.

JURISDICTION OF THE SUBJECT MATTER

The District Court was uncertain whether our cases withholding federal judicial relief rested upon a lack of federal jurisdiction or upon the inappropriateness of the subject matter for judicial consideration—what we have designated "nonjusticiability." The distinction between the two grounds is significant. In the instance of nonjusticiability, consideration of the cause is not wholly and immediately foreclosed; rather, the Court's inquiry necessarily proceeds to the point of deciding whether the duty asserted can be judicially identified and its breach judicially determined, and whether protection for the right asserted can be judicially molded. In the instance of lack of jurisdiction the cause either does not "arise under" the Federal Constitution, laws or treaties (or fall within one of the other enumerated categories of Art. III, § 2), or is not a "case or controversy" within the meaning of that section; or the cause is not one described by any jurisdictional statute. Our conclusion, that this cause presents no nonjusticiable "political question" settles the only possible doubt that it is a case or controversy. Under the present heading of "Jurisdiction of the Subject Matter" we hold only that the matter set forth in the complaint does arise under the Constitution and is within 28 U.S.C. § 1343.

Article III, § 2 of the Federal Constitution provides that "the judicial Power shall extend to all Cases, in Law and Equity, arising under this Constitution, the Laws of the United States, and Treaties made, or which shall be made, under their Authority; . . ." It is clear that the cause of action is one which "arises under" the Federal Constitution. The complaint alleges that the 1901 statute effects an apportionment that deprives the appellants of the equal protection of the laws in violation of the Fourteenth Amendment. . . .

The appellees refer to *Colegrove v. Green*, 328 U.S. 549, as authority that the District Court lacked jurisdiction of the subject matter. Appellees misconceive the holding of that case. The holding was precisely contrary to their reading of it. Seven members of the Court participated in the decision. Unlike many other cases in this field which have assumed without discussion that there was jurisdiction, all three opinions filed in *Colegrove* discussed the question.

Two of the opinions expressing the views of four of the Justices, a majority, flatly held that there was jurisdiction of the subject matter. . . .

STANDING

A federal court cannot "pronounce any statute, either of a State or of the United States, void, because irreconcilable with the Constitution, except as it is called upon to adjudge the legal rights of litigants in actual controversies." *Liverpool Steamship Co. v. Commissioners of Emigration*, 113 U.S. 33, 39. Have the appellants alleged such a personal stake in the outcome of the controversy as to assure that concrete adverseness which sharpens the presentation of issues upon which the court so largely depends for illumination of difficult constitutional questions? This is the gist of the question of standing. It is, of course, a question of federal law.

The complaint was filed by residents of Davidson, Hamilton, Knox, Montgomery, and Shelby Counties. Each is a person allegedly qualified to vote for members of the General Assembly representing his county. . . .

We hold that the appellants do have standing to maintain this suit. . . .

These appellants seek relief in order to protect or vindicate an interest of their own, and of those similarly situated. Their constitutional claim is, in substance, that the 1901 statute constitutes arbitrary and capricious state action, offensive to the Fourteenth Amendment in its irrational disregard of the standard of apportionment prescribed by the State's Constitution or of any standard, effecting a gross disproportion of representation to voting population. The injury which appellants assert is that this classification disfavors the voters in the counties in which they reside, placing them in a position of constitutionally unjustifiable inequality *vis-à-vis* voters in irrationally favored counties. A citizen's right to a vote free of arbitrary impairment by state action has been judicially recognized as a right secured by the Constitution, when such impairment resulted from dilution by a false tally, cf. *United States v. Classic*, 313 U.S. 299; or by a refusal to count votes from arbitrarily selected precincts, cf. *United States v. Mosley*, 238 U.S. 383, or by a stuffing of the ballot box, cf. *Ex parte Siebold*, 100 U.S. 371; *United States v. Saylor*, 322 U.S. 385.

It would not be necessary to decide whether appellants'

allegations of impairment of their votes by the 1901 apportionment will, ultimately, entitle them to any relief, in order to hold that they have standing to seek it. If such impairment does produce a legally cognizable injury, they are among those who have sustained it. . . .

JUSTICIABILITY

In holding that the subject matter of this suit was not justiciable, the District Court relied on *Colegrove v. Green*, *supra*, and subsequent *per curiam* cases. The court stated: "From a review of these decisions there can be no doubt that the federal rule . . . is that the federal courts . . . will not intervene in cases of this type to compel legislative reapportionment." 179 F. Supp., at 826. We understand the District Court to have read the cited cases as compelling the conclusion that since the appellants sought to have a legislative apportionment held unconstitutional, their suit presented a "political question" and was therefore nonjusticiable. We hold that this challenge to an apportionment presents no nonjusticiable "political question." The cited cases do not hold the contrary.

Of course the mere fact that the suit seeks protection of a political right does not mean it presents a political question. Such an objection "is little more than a play upon words." *Nixon v. Herndon*, 273 U.S. 536, 540. Rather, it is argued that apportionment cases, whatever the actual wording of the complaint, can involve no federal constitutional right except one resting on the guaranty of a republican form of government, and that complaints based on that clause have been held to present political questions which are nonjusticiable.

We hold that the claim pleaded here neither rests upon nor implicates the Guaranty Clause and that its justiciability is therefore not foreclosed by our decisions of cases involving that clause . . .

Our discussion, even at the price of extending this opinion, requires review of a number of political question cases, in order to expose the attributes of the doctrine—attributes which, in various settings, diverge, combine, appear, and disappear in seeming disorderliness. Since that review is undertaken solely to demonstrate that neither singly nor collectively do these cases support a conclusion that this apportionment case is nonjusticiable, we of course do not explore their implications in other contexts. That review reveals that in the Guaranty Clause cases and in the other "political question" cases, it is the relationship between the judiciary and the coordinate branches of the Federal Government, and not the federal judiciary's relationship to the States, which gives rise to the "political question."

We have said that "in determining whether a question falls within [the political question] category, the appropriateness under our system of government of attributing finality to the action of the political departments and also the lack of satisfactory criteria for a judicial determination are dominant considerations." *Coleman v. Miller*, 307 U.S. 433, 454–455. The nonjusticiability of a political question is primarily a function of the separation of powers. Much confusion results from the capacity of the "political question" label to obscure the need for case-by-case inquiry. Deciding whether a matter has in any measure been committed by the Constitution to another branch of government, or whether the action of that branch exceeds whatever authority has been committed, is itself a delicate exercise in constitutional interpretation, and is a responsibility of this Court as ultimate interpreter of the Constitution. To demonstrate this requires no less than to analyze representative cases and to infer from them the analytical threads that make up the political question doctrine. We shall then show that none of those threads catches this case. . . .

It is apparent that several formulations which vary slightly according to the settings in which the questions arise may describe a political question, although each has one or more elements which identifies it as essentially a function of the separation of powers. Prominent on the surface of any case held to involve a political question is found a textually demonstrable constitutional commitment of the issue to a coordinate political department; or a lack of judicially discoverable and manageable standards for resolving it; or the impossibility of deciding without an initial policy determination of a kind clearly for nonjudicial discretion; or the impossibility of a court's undertaking independent resolution without expressing lack of the respect due coordinate branches of government; or an unusual need for unquestioning adherence to a political decision already made; or the potentiality of embarrassment from multifarious pronouncements by various departments on one question.

Unless one of these formulations is inextricable from the case at bar, there should be no dismissal for nonjusticiability on the ground of a political question's presence. The doctrine of which we treat is one of "political questions," not of "political cases." The courts cannot reject as "no law suit" a bona fide controversy as to whether some action denominated "political" exceeds constitutional authority. The cases we have reviewed show the necessity for discriminatory inquiry into the precise facts and posture of the particular case, and the impossibility of resolution by any semantic cataloguing.

But it is argued that this case shares the characteristics of decisions that constitute a category not yet considered, cases concerning the Constitution's guaranty in Art. 4, § 4, of a republican form of government. A conclusion as to whether the case at bar does present a political question cannot be confidently reached until we have considered those cases with special care. We shall discover that Guaranty Clause claims involve those elements which define a "political question," and for that reason and no other, they are nonjusticiable. In particular, we shall discover that the nonjusticiability of such claims has nothing to do with their touching upon matters of state governmental organization. . . .

We come, finally, to the ultimate inquiry whether our precedents as to what constitutes a nonjusticiable "political question" bring the case before us under the umbrella of that doctrine. A natural beginning is to note whether any of the common characteristics which we have been able to identify and label descriptively are present. We find none: The question here is the consistency of state action with the Federal Constitution. We have no question decided, or to be decided, by a political branch of government coequal with this Court. Nor do we risk embarrassment of our government abroad, or grave disturbance at home if we take issue with Tennessee as to the constitutionality of her action here challenged. Nor need the appellants, in order to succeed in this action, ask the Court to enter upon policy determinations for which judicially manageable standards are lacking. Judicial standards under the Equal Protection Clause are well developed and familiar, and it has been open to courts since the enactment of the Fourteenth Amendment to determine, if on the particular facts they must, that a discrimination reflects *no* policy, but simply arbitrary and capricious action.

This case does, in one sense, involve the allocation of political power within a State, and the appellants might conceivably have added a claim under the Guaranty Clause. Of course, as we have seen, any reliance on that clause would be futile. But because any reliance on the Guaranty Clause could not have succeeded it does not follow that appellants may not be heard on the equal protection claim which in fact they tender. True, it must be clear that the Fourteenth Amendment claim is not so enmeshed with those political question elements which render Guaranty Clause claims nonjusticiable as actually to present a political question itself. But we have found that not to be the case here. . . .

When challenges to state action respecting matters of "the administration of the affairs of the State and the officers through whom they are conducted" have rested on claims of constitutional deprivation which are amenable to judicial correction, this Court has acted upon its view of the merits of the claim. For example, in *Boyd v. Nebraska ex rel. Thayer,* 143 U.S. 135, we reversed the Nebraska Supreme Court's decision that Nebraska's Governor was not a citizen of the United States or of the State and therefore could not continue in office. In *Kennard v. Louisiana ex rel. Morgan,* 92 U.S. (2 Otto) 480, and *Foster v. Kansas ex rel. Johnston,* 112 U.S. 201, we considered whether persons had been removed from public office by procedures consistent with the Fourteenth Amendment's due process guaranty, and held on the merits that they had. And only last Term, in *Gomillion v. Lightfoot,* 364 U.S. 339, we applied the Fifteenth Amendment to strike down a redrafting of municipal boundaries which effected a discriminatory impairment of voting rights, in the face of what a majority of the Court of Appeals thought to be a sweeping commitment to state legislatures of the power to draw and redraw such boundaries.

Gomillion was brought by a Negro, who had been a resident of the City of Tuskegee, Alabama, until the municipal boundaries were so recast by the State Legislature as to exclude practically all Negroes. The plaintiff claimed deprivation of the right to vote in municipal elections. The District Court's dismissal for want of jurisdiction and failure to state a claim upon which relief could be granted was affirmed by the Court of Appeals. This Court unanimously reversed. . . .

We conclude that the complaint's allegations of a denial of equal protection present a justiciable constitutional cause of action upon which appellants are entitled to a trial and a decision. The right asserted is within the reach of judicial protection under the Fourteenth Amendment.

The judgment of the District Court is reversed and the cause is remanded for further proceedings consistent with this opinion.

Reversed and remanded.

MR. JUSTICE DOUGLAS, *concurring.*

While I join the opinion of the Court and, like the Court, do not reach the merits, a word of explanation is necessary. I put to one side the problems of "political" questions involving the distribution of power between this Court, the Congress, and the Chief Executive. We have here a phase of the recurring problem of the relation of the federal courts to state agencies. More particularly, the question is the extent to which a State may weight one person's vote more heavily than it does another's. . . .

There is a third barrier to a State's freedom in prescribing qualifications of voters and that is the Equal Protection Clause of the Fourteenth Amendment, the provision invoked here. And so the question is, may a State weight the vote of one county or one district more heavily than it weights the vote in another?

The traditional test under the Equal Protection Clause has been whether a State has made "an invidious discrimination," as it does when it selects "a particular race or nationality for oppressive treatment." See *Skinner v. Oklahoma*, 316 U.S. 535, 541. Universal equality is not the test; there is room for weighting. As we stated in *Williamson v. Lee Optical Co.*, 348 U.S. 483, 489, "The prohibition of the Equal Protection Clause goes no further than the invidious discrimination." . . .

With the exceptions of *Colegrove v. Green*, 328 U.S. 549; *MacDougall v. Green*, 335 U.S. 281; *South v. Peters*, 339 U.S. 276, and the decisions they spawned, the Court has never thought that protection of voting rights was beyond judicial cognizance of the claims stated in the present complaint.

The justiciability of the present claims being established, any relief accorded can be fashioned in the light of well-known principles of equity.

MR. JUSTICE CLARK, *concurring.*

One emerging from the rash of opinions with their accompanying clashing of views may well find himself suffering a mental blindness. The Court holds that the appellants have alleged a cause of action. However, it refuses to award relief here—although the facts are undisputed—and fails to give the District Court any guidance whatever. One dissenting opinion, bursting with words that go through so much and conclude with so little, contemns the majority action as "a massive repudiation of the experience of our whole past." Another describes the complaint as merely asserting conclusory allegations that Tennessee's apportionment is "incorrect," "arbitrary," "obsolete," and "unconstitutional." I believe it can be shown that this case is distinguishable from earlier cases dealing with the distribution of political power by a State, that a patent violation of the Equal Protection Clause of the United States Constitution has been shown, and that an appropriate remedy may be formulated. . . .

The controlling facts cannot be disputed. It appears from the record that 37 percent of the voters of Tennessee elect 20 of the 33 Senators while 40 percent of the voters elect 63 of the 99 members of the House. But this might not on its face be an "invidious discrimination," *Williamson v. Lee Optical of Oklahoma*, 348 U.S. 483, 489 (1955), for a "statutory discrimination will not be set aside if any state of facts reasonably may be conceived to justify it." *McGowan v. Maryland*, 366 U.S. 420, 426 (1961).

It is true that the apportionment policy incorporated in Tennessee's Constitution, i.e., state-wide numerical equality of representation with certain minor qualifications, is a rational one. On a county-by-county comparison a districting plan based thereon naturally will have disparities in representation due to the qualifications. But this to my mind does not raise constitutional problems, for the overall policy is reasonable. However, the root of the trouble is not in Tennessee's Constitution, for admittedly its policy has not been followed. The discrimination lies in the action of Tennessee's Assembly in allocating legislative seats to counties or districts created by it. Try as one may, Tennessee's apportionment just cannot be made to fit the pattern cut by its

Constitution. . . . Tennessee's apportionment is a crazy quilt without rational basis. . . .

The truth is that—although this case has been here for two years and has had over six hours' argument (three times the ordinary case) and has been most carefully considered over and over again by us in Conference and individually—no one, not even the State nor the dissenters, has come up with any rational basis for Tennessee's apportionment statute. . . .

Although I find the Tennessee apportionment statute offends the Equal Protection Clause, I would not consider intervention by this Court into so delicate a field if there were any other relief available to the people of Tennessee. But the majority of the people of Tennessee have no "practical opportunities for exerting their political weight at the polls" to correct the existing "invidious discrimination." Tennessee has no initiative and referendum. I have searched diligently for other "practical opportunities" present under the law. I find none other than through the federal courts. The majority of the voters have been caught up in a legislative strait jacket. Tennessee has an "informed, civically militant electorate" and "an aroused popular conscience," but it does not sear "the conscience of the people's representatives." This is because the legislative policy has riveted the present seats in the Assembly to their respective constituencies, and by the votes of their incumbents a reapportionment of any kind is prevented. The people have been rebuffed at the hands of the Assembly; they have tried the constitutional convention route, but since the call must originate in the Assembly it, too, has been fruitless. They have tried Tennessee courts with the same result, and Governors have fought the tide only to flounder. It is said that there is recourse in Congress and perhaps that may be, but from a practical standpoint this is without substance. To date Congress has never undertaken such a task in any State. We therefore must conclude that the people of Tennessee are stymied and without judicial intervention will be saddled with the present discrimination in the affairs of their state government.

Finally, we must consider if there are any appropriate modes of effective judicial relief. The federal courts are, of course, not forums for political debate, nor should they resolve themselves into state constitutional conventions or legislative assemblies. Nor should their jurisdiction be exercised in the hope that such a declaration, as is made today, may have the direct effect of bringing on legislative action and relieving the courts of the problem of fashioning relief. To my mind this would be nothing less than blackjacking the Assembly into reapportioning the State. If judicial competence were lacking to fashion an effective decree, I would dismiss this appeal. However, like the Solicitor General of the United States, I see no such difficulty in the position of this case. One plan might be to start with the existing assembly districts, consolidate some of them, and award the seats thus released to those counties suffering the most egregious discrimination. Other possibilities are present and might be more effective. But the plan here suggested would at least release the strangle hold now on the Assembly and permit it to redistrict itself. . . .

As John Rutledge (later Chief Justice) said 175 years ago in the course of the Constitutional Convention, a chief function of the Court is to secure the national rights. Its decision today supports the proposition for which our forebears fought and many died, namely that "to be fully conformable to the principle of right, the form of government must be representative." That is the keystone upon which our government was founded and lacking which no republic can survive. It is well for this Court to practice self-restraint and discipline in constitutional adjudication, but never in its history have those principles received sanction where the national rights of so many have been so clearly infringed for so long a time. National respect for the courts is more enhanced through the forthright enforcement of those rights rather than by rendering them nugatory through the interposition of subterfuges. In my view the ultimate decision today is in the greatest tradition of this Court.

MR. JUSTICE STEWART, *concurring.*

The separate writings of my dissenting and concurring Brothers stray so far from the subject of today's decision as to convey, I think, a distressingly inaccurate impression of what the Court decides. For that reason, I think it appropriate, in joining the opinion of the Court, to emphasize in a few words what the opinion does and does not say.

The Court today decides three things and no more: "(a) that the court possessed jurisdiction of the subject matter; (b) that a justiciable cause of action is stated upon which appellants would be entitled to appropriate relief; and (c) . . . that the appellants have standing to challenge the Tennessee apportionment statutes."

The complaint in this case asserts that Tennessee's system of apportionment is utterly arbitrary—without any possible justification in rationality. The District Court did not reach the merits of that claim, and this Court quite properly expresses no view on the subject. Contrary to the suggestion of my Brother HARLAN, the Court does not say or imply that "state legislatures must be so structured as to reflect with approximate equality the voice of every voter." The Court does not say or imply that there is anything in the Federal Constitution "to prevent a State, acting not irrationally, from choosing any electoral legislative structure it thinks best suited to the interests, temper, and customs of its people." And contrary to the suggestion of my Brother DOUGLAS, the Court most assuredly does not decide the question, "may a State weight the vote of one county or one district more heavily than it weights the vote in another?" . . .

MR. JUSTICE FRANKFURTER, *whom* MR. JUSTICE HARLAN *joins, dissenting.*

The Court today reverses a uniform course of decision established by a dozen cases, including one by which the very claim now sustained was unanimously rejected only five years ago. The impressive body of rulings thus cast aside reflected the equally uniform course of our political history regarding the relationship between population and legislative representation—a wholly different matter from denial of the franchise to individuals because of race, color, religion or sex. Such a massive repudiation of the experience of our whole past in asserting destructively novel judicial power demands a detailed analysis of the role of this Court in our constitutional scheme. Disregard of inherent limits in the effective exercise of the Court's "judicial Power" not only presages the futility of judicial intervention in the essentially political conflict of forces by which the relation between population and representation has time out of mind been and now is determined. It may well impair the Court's position as the ultimate organ of "the supreme Law of the Land" in that vast range of legal problems, often strongly entangled in popular feeling, on which this Court must pronounce. The Court's authority—possessed neither of the purse nor the sword—ultimately rests on sustained public confidence in its moral sanction. Such feeling must be nourished by the Court's complete detachment, in fact and in appearance, from political entanglements and by abstention from injecting itself into the clash of political forces in political settlements.

A hypothetical claim resting on abstract assumptions is now for the first time made the basis for affording illusory relief for a particular evil even though it foreshadows deeper and more pervasive difficulties in consequence. The claim is hypothetical and the assumptions are abstract because the Court does not vouchsafe the lower courts—state and federal—guide-lines for formulating specific, definite, wholly unprecedented remedies for the inevitable litigations that today's umbrageous disposition is bound to stimulate in connection with politically motivated reapportionments in so many States. In such a setting, to promulgate jurisdiction in the abstract is meaningless. It is devoid of reality as "a brooding omnipresence in the sky" for it conveys no intimation what relief, if any, a District Court is capable of affording that would not invite legislatures to play ducks and drakes with the judiciary. For this Court to direct the District Court to enforce a claim to which the Court has over the years consistently found itself required to deny legal enforcement and at the same time to find it necessary to withhold any guidance to the lower court how to enforce this turnabout, new legal claim, manifests an odd—indeed an esoteric—conception of judicial propriety. One of the Court's supporting opinions, as elucidated by commentary, unwittingly affords a disheartening preview of the mathematical quagmire (apart from divers judicially inappropriate and elusive determinants), into which this Court today catapults the lower courts of the country without so much as adumbrating the basis for a legal calculus as a means of extrication. Even assuming the indispensable intellectual disinterestedness on the part of judges in such matters, they do not have accepted legal standards or criteria or even reliable analogies to draw upon for making judicial judgments. To charge courts with the task of accommodating the incommensurable factors of policy that underlie these mathematical puzzles is to attribute, however flatteringly, omnicompetence to judges. The Framers of the Constitution persistently rejected a proposal that embodied this assumption and Thomas Jefferson never entertained it.

Recent legislation, creating a district appropriately described as "an atrocity of ingenuity," is not unique. Considering the gross inequality among legislative electoral units within almost every State, the Court naturally shrinks from asserting that in districting at least substantial equality is a constitutional requirement enforceable by courts. Room continues to be allowed for weighting. This of course implies that geography, economics, urban-rural conflict, and all the other non-legal factors which have throughout our history entered into political districting are to some extent not to be ruled out in the undefined vista now opened up by review in the federal courts of state reapportionments. To some extent—aye, there's the rub. In effect, today's decision empowers the courts of the country to devise what should constitute the proper composition of the legislatures of the fifty States. If state courts should for one reason or another find themselves unable to discharge this task, the duty of doing so is put on the federal courts or on this Court, if State views do not satisfy this Court's notion of what is proper districting.

We were soothingly told at the bar of this Court that we need not worry about the kind of remedy a court could effectively fashion once the abstract constitutional right to have courts pass on a state-wide system of electoral districting is recognized as a matter of judicial rhetoric, because legislatures would heed the Court's admonition. This is not only an euphoric hope. It implies a sorry confession of judicial impotence in place of a frank acknowledgment that there is not under our Constitution a judicial remedy for every political mischief, for every undesirable exercise of legislative power. The Framers carefully and with deliberate forethought refused so to enthrone the judiciary. In this situation, as in others of like nature, appeal for relief does not belong here. Appeal must be to an informed, civically militant electorate. In a democratic society like ours, relief must come through an aroused popular conscience that sears the conscience of the people's representatives. In any event there is nothing judicially more unseemly nor more self-defeating than for this Court to make *in terrorem* pronouncements, to indulge in merely empty rhetoric, sounding a word of promise to the ear, sure to be disappointing to the hope. . . .

In sustaining appellants' claim, based on the Fourteenth Amendment, that the District Court may entertain this suit, this Court's uniform course of decision over the years is overruled or disregarded. Explicitly it begins with *Colegrove v. Green, supra,* decided in 1946, but its roots run deep in the Court's historic adjudicatory process.

Colegrove held that a federal court should not entertain an action for declaratory and injunctive relief to adjudicate the constitutionality, under the Equal Protection Clause and other federal constitutional and statutory provisions, of a state statute establishing the respective districts for the State's election of Representatives to the Congress. Two opinions were written by the four Justices who composed the majority of the seven sitting members of the Court. Both opinions joining in the result in *Colegrove v. Green* agreed that considerations were controlling which dictated denial of jurisdiction though not in the strict sense of want of power. While the two opinions show a divergence of view regarding some of these considerations, there are important points of concurrence. Both opinions demonstrate a predominant concern, first, with avoiding federal judicial involvement in matters traditionally left to legislative policy-making; second, with respect to the difficulty—in view of the nature of the problems of apportionment and its history in this country—of drawing on or devising judicial standards for judgment, as opposed to legislative determinations, of the part which mere numerical equality among voters should play as a criterion for the allocation of political power; and, third, with problems of finding appropriate modes of relief—particularly, the problem of resolving the essentially political issue of the relative merits of at-large elections and elections held in districts of unequal population.

The broad applicability of these considerations—summarized in the loose shorthand phrase, "political question"—in cases involving a State's apportionment of voting power among its numerous localities has led the Court, since 1946, to recognize their controlling effect in a variety of situations. . . .

The present case involves all of the elements that have made the Guarantee Clause cases nonjusticiable. It is, in effect, a Guarantee Clause claim masquerading under a different label. But it cannot make the case more fit for judicial action that appellants invoke the Fourteenth Amendment rather than Art. IV, § 4, where, in fact, the gist of their complaint is the same—unless it can be found that the Fourteenth Amendment speaks with greater particularity to their situation. We have been admonished to avoid "the tyranny of labels." *Snyder v. Massachusetts*, 291, U.S. 97, 114. Art. IV, § 4, is not committed by express constitutional terms to Congress. It is the nature of the controversies arising under it, nothing else, which has made it judicially unenforceable. . . .

What, then, is this question of legislative apportionment? Appellants invoke the right to vote and to have their votes counted. But they are permitted to vote and their votes are counted. They go to the polls, they cast their ballots, they send their representatives to the state councils. Their complaint is simply that the representatives are not sufficiently numerous or powerful—in short, that Tennessee has adopted a basis of representation with which they are dissatisfied. Talk of "debasement" or "dilution" is circular talk. One cannot speak of "debasement" or "dilution" of the value of a vote until there is first defined a standard of reference as to what a vote should be worth. What is actually asked of the Court in this case is to choose among competing bases of representation—ultimately, really, among competing theories of political philosophy—in order to establish an appropriate frame of government for the State of Tennessee and thereby for all the States of the Union. . . .

The notion that representation proportioned to the geographic spread of population is so universally accepted as a necessary element of equality between man and man that it must be taken to be the standard of a political equality preserved by the Fourteenth Amendment—that it is, in appellants' words "the basic principle of representative government"—is, to put it bluntly, not true. However desirable and however desired by some among the great political thinkers and framers of our government, it has never been generally practiced, today or in the past. It was not the English system, it was not the colonial system, it was not the system chosen for the national government by the Constitution, it was not the system exclusively or even predominantly practiced by the States at the time of adoption of the Fourteenth Amendment, it is not predominantly practiced by the States today. Unless judges, the judges of this Court, are to make their private views of political wisdom the measure of the Constitution—views which in all honesty cannot but give the appearance, if not reflect the reality, of involvement with the business of partisan politics so inescapably a part of apportionment controversies—the Fourteenth Amendment, "itself a historical product," *Jackman v. Rosenbaum Co.*, 260 U.S. 22, 31, provides no guide for judicial oversight of the representation problem. . . .

Contemporary apportionment. Detailed recent studies are available to describe the present-day constitutional and statutory status of apportionment in the fifty States. They demonstrate a decided twentieth-century trend away from population as the exclusive base of representation. Today, only a dozen state constitutions provide for periodic legislative reapportionment of both houses by a substantially unqualified application of the population standard, and only about a dozen more prescribe such reapportionment for even a single chamber. "Specific provision for county representation in at least one house of the state legislature has been increasingly adopted since the end of the nineteenth century. . . ." More than twenty States now guarantee each county at least one seat in one of their houses regardless of population, and in nine others county or town units are given equal representation in one legislative branch, whatever the number of each unit's inhabitants. Of course, numerically considered, "These provisions invariably result in overrepresentation of the least populated areas. . . ." And in an effort to curb the political dominance of metropolitan regions, at least ten States now limit the maximum entitlement of any single county (or, in some cases, city) in one legislative house—another source of substantial numerical disproportion.

Moreover, it is common knowledge that the legislatures have not kept reapportionment up to date, even where state constitutions in terms require it. In particular, the pattern of according greater per capita representation to rural, relatively sparsely populated areas—the same pattern which finds expression in various state constitutional provisions, and which has been given effect in England and elsewhere—has, in some of the States been made the law by legislative inaction in the face of population shifts. Throughout the country, urban and suburban areas tend to be given higher representation ratios than do rural areas.

The stark fact is that if among the numerous widely varying principles and practices that control state legislative apportionment today there is any generally prevailing feature, that feature is geographic inequality in relation to the population standard. Examples could be endlessly multiplied. . . .

Manifestly, the Equal Protection Clause supplies no clearer guide for judicial examination of apportionment methods than would the Guarantee Clause itself. Apportionment, by its character, is a subject of extraordinary complexity, involving—even after the fundamental theoretical issues concerning what is to be represented in a representative legislature have been fought out or compromised—considerations of geography, demography, electoral convenience, economic and social cohesions or divergencies among particular local groups, communications, the practical effects of political institutions like the lobby and the city machine, ancient traditions and ties of settled usage, respect for proven incumbents of long experience and senior status, mathematical mechanics, censuses compiling relevant data, and a host of others. Legislative responses throughout the country to the reapportionment demands of the 1960 Census have glaringly confirmed that these are not factors that lend themselves to evaluations of a nature that are the staple of judicial determinations or for which judges are equipped to adjudicate by legal training or experience or native wit. And this is the more so true because in every strand of this complicated, intricate web of values meet the contending forces of partisan politics. The practical significance of apportionment is that the next election results may differ because of it. Apportionment battles are overwhelmingly party or intra-party contests. It will add a virulent source of friction and tension in federal-state relations to embroil the federal judiciary in them. . . .

Wesberry v. Sanders (376 U.S. 1)
Decided February 17, 1964

Mr. Justice Black *delivered the opinion of the Court.*

Appellants are citizens and qualified voters of Fulton County, Georgia, and as such are entitled to vote in congressional elections in Georgia's Fifth Congressional District. That district, one of ten created by a 1931 Georgia statute, includes Fulton, DeKalb, and Rockdale Counties and has a population according to the 1960 census of 823,680. The average population of the ten districts is 394,312, less than half that of the Fifth. One district, the Ninth, has only 272,154 people, less than one-third as many as the Fifth. . . . The complaint alleged that appellants were deprived of the full benefit of their right to vote, in violation of (1) Art. I, § 2 of the Constitution of the United States, which provides that "The House of Representatives shall be composed of Members chosen every second year by the People of the several States . . ."; (2) the Due Process, Equal Protection, and Privileges and Immunities Clauses of the Fourteenth Amendment; and (3) that part of Section 2 of the Fourteenth Amendment which provides that "Representatives shall be apportioned among the several States according to their respective numbers. . . ."

The case was heard by a three-judge District Court, which found unanimously, from facts not disputed, that:

> It is clear by any standard . . . that the population of the Fifth District is grossly out of balance with that of the other nine congressional districts of Georgia and in fact, so much so that the removal of DeKalb and Rockdale Counties from the District, leaving only Fulton with a population of 556,326, would leave it exceeding the average by slightly more than 40 percent.

Notwithstanding these findings, a majority of the court dismissed the complaint, citing as their guide Mr. Justice

Frankfurter's minority opinion in *Colegrove v. Green*, 328 U.S. 549, an opinion stating that challenges to apportionment of congressional districts raised only "political" questions, which were not justiciable. . . . [In] debasing the weight of appellants' votes the State has abridged the right to vote for members of Congress guaranteed them by the United States Constitution. . . . The question of what relief should be given we leave for further consideration and decision by the District Court in light of existing circumstances. . . .

[The] statement in *Baker* [*v. Carr*] which referred to our past decisions holding congressional apportionment cases to be justiciable, we believe was wholly correct and we adhere to it. Mr. Justice Frankfurter's *Colegrove* opinion contended that Art. I, § 4, of the Constitution had given Congress "exclusive authority" to protect the right of citizens to vote for congressmen, but we made it clear in *Baker* that nothing in the language of that article gives support to a construction that would immunize state congressional apportionment laws which debase a citizen's right to vote from the power of courts to protect the constitutional rights of individuals from legislative destruction. . . . The right to vote is too important in our free society to be stripped of judicial protection by such an interpretation of Article I. This dismissal can no more be justified on the ground of "want of equity" than on the ground of "nonjusticiability." We therefore hold that the District Court erred in dismissing the complaint. . . .

We agree with the District Court that the 1931 Georgia apportionment grossly discriminated against voters in the Fifth Congressional District. A single congressman represents from two to three times as many fifth district voters as are represented by each of the congressmen from the other Georgia congressional districts. The apportionment statute thus contracts the value of some votes and expands that of others. If the Federal Constitution intends that when qualified voters elect members of Congress each vote be given as much weight as any other vote, then this statute cannot stand.

We hold that, construed in its historical context, the command of Art. I, § 2 that Representatives be chosen "by the People of the several States" means that as nearly as is practicable one man's vote in a congressional election is to be worth as much as another's.* This rule is followed automatically, of course, when Representatives are chosen as a group on a statewide basis, as was a widespread practice in the first fifty years of our Nation's history. It would be extraordinary to suggest that in such statewide elections the votes of inhabitants of some parts of a State, for example, Georgia's thinly populated ninth district, could be weighed at two or three times the value of the votes of people living in more populous parts of the State, for example, the Fifth district around Atlanta. Cf. *Gray v. Sanders*, 372 U.S. 368. We do not believe that the Framers of the Constitution intended to permit the same vote-diluting discrimination to be accomplished through the device of districts containing widely varied numbers of inhabitants. To say that a vote is worth more in one district than in another would not only run counter to our fundamental ideas of democratic government, it would cast aside the principle of a House of Representatives elected "by the People," a principle tenaciously fought for and established at the Constitutional Convention. The history of the Constitution, particularly that part of it relating to the adoption of Art. I, § 2, reveals that those who framed the Constitution meant that, no matter what the mechanics of an election, whether statewide or by districts, it was population which was to be the basis of the House of Representatives. . . .

It is in the light of such history that we must construe Art. I, § 2, of the Constitution, which, carrying out the ideas of Madison and those of like views, provides that Representatives shall be chosen "by the People of the several States" and shall be "apportioned among the several States . . . according to their respective Numbers." It is not surprising that our Court has held that this article gives persons qualified to vote a constitutional right to vote and to have their votes counted. . . . No right is more precious in a free country than that of having a voice in the election of those who make the laws under which, as good citizens, we must live. Other rights, even the most basic, are illusory if the right to vote is undermined. Our Constitution leaves no room for classification of people in a way that unnecessarily

* We do not reach the argument that the Georgia statute violates the Due Process, Equal Protection, and Privileges and Immunities Clauses of the Fourteenth Amendment.

abridges this right. In urging the people to adopt the Constitution, Madison said in No. 57 of *The Federalist:*

> Who are to be the electors of the Foederal Representatives? Not the rich more than the poor; not the learned more than the ignorant; not the haughty heirs of distinguished names, more than the humble sons of obscure and unpropitious fortune. The electors are to be the great body of the people of the United States. . . .

Readers surely could have fairly taken this to mean, "one person, one vote." Cf. *Gray v. Sanders*, 372 U.S. 368, 381.

While it may not be possible to draw congressional districts with mathematical precision, that is no excuse for ignoring our Constitution's plain objective of making equal representation for equal numbers of people the fundamental goal for the House of Representatives. That is the high standard of justice and common sense which the Founders set for us.

Revised and remanded.

MR. JUSTICE CLARK, *concurring in part and dissenting in part.*

Unfortunately I can join neither the opinion of the Court nor the dissent of my Brother HARLAN. It is true that the opening sentence of Art. I, § 2, of the Constitution provides that Representatives are to be chosen "by the People of the several States. . . ." However, in my view, Brother HARLAN has clearly demonstrated that both the historical background and language preclude a finding that Art. I, § 2, lays down the *ipse dixit* "one person, one vote" in congressional elections.

On the other hand, I agree with the majority that congressional districting is subject to judicial scrutiny. This Court has so held ever since *Smiley v. Holm*, 285 U.S. 355 (1932), which is buttressed by two companion cases, *Koenig v. Flynn*, 285 U.S. 375 (1932), and *Carroll v. Becker*, 285 U.S. 380 (1932). A majority of the Court in *Colegrove v. Green* felt, upon the authority of *Smiley*, that the complaint presented a justiciable controversy not reserved exclusively to Congress. *Colegrove v. Green*, 328 U.S. 549, 564, and 568, n. 3 (1946). Again, in *Baker v. Carr*, 369 U.S. 186, 232 (1962), the opinion of the Court recognized that *Smiley* "settled the issue in favor of justiciability of questions of congressional redistricting." I therefore cannot agree with Brother HARLAN that the supervisory power granted to Congress under Art. I, § 4, is the exclusive remedy.

I would examine the Georgia congressional districts against the requirements of the Equal Protection Clause of the Fourteenth Amendment. As my Brother BLACK said in his dissent in *Colegrove v. Green, supra,* the "equal protection clause of the Fourteenth Amendment forbids . . . discrimination. It does not permit the States to pick out certain qualified citizens or groups of citizens and deny them the right to vote at all. . . . No one would deny that the equal protection clause would also prohibit a law that would expressly give certain citizens a half-vote and others a full vote. . . . Such discriminatory legislation seems to me exactly the kind that the equal protection clause was intended to prohibit." At 569.

The trial court, however, did not pass upon the merits of the case, although it does appear that it did make a finding that the Fifth District of Georgia was "grossly out of balance" with other congressional districts of the State. Instead of proceeding on the merits, the court dismissed the case for lack of equity. I believe that the court erred in so doing. In my view we should therefore vacate this judgment and remand the case for a hearing on the merits. At that hearing the court should apply the standards laid down in *Baker v. Carr, supra.*

I would have an additional caveat. The General Assembly of the Georgia Legislature has been recently reapportioned as a result of the order of the three-judge District Court in *Toombs v. Fortson,* 205 F. Supp. 248 (1962). In addition, the Assembly has created a Joint Congressional Redistricting Study Committee which has been working on the problem of congressional redistricting for several months. The General Assembly is currently in session. If on remand the trial court is of the opinion that there is likelihood of the General Assembly reapportioning the State in an appropriate manner, I believe that coercive relief should be deferred until after the General Assembly has had such an opportunity.

MR. JUSTICE HARLAN, *dissenting.*

I had not expected to witness the day when the Supreme Court of the United States would render a decision which casts grave doubt on the constitutionality of the composition of the House of Representatives. It is not an exaggeration to say that such is the effect of today's decision. The Court's holding that the Constitution requires States to select Representatives either by elections at large or by elections in districts composed "as nearly as is practicable" of equal population places in jeopardy the seats of almost all the members of the present House of Representatives.

In the last congressional election, in 1962, Representatives from 42 States were elected from congressional districts. In all but five of those States, the difference between the populations of the largest and smallest districts exceeded 100,000 persons. A difference of this magnitude in the size of districts the average population of which in each State is less than 500,000 is presumably not equality among districts "as nearly as is practicable," although the Court does not reveal its definition of that phrase. Thus, today's decision impugns the validity of the election of 398 Representatives from 37 States, leaving a "constitutional" House of 37 members now sitting.

Only a demonstration which could not be avoided would justify this Court in rendering a decision the effect of which, inescapably as I see it, is to declare constitutionally defective the very composition of a coordinate branch of the Federal Government. The Court's opinion not only fails to make such a demonstration. It is unsound logically on its face and demonstrably unsound historically.

Before coming to grips with the reasoning that carried such extraordinary consequences, it is important to have firmly in mind the provisions of Article I of the Constitution which control this case.

> Section 2. The House of Representatives shall be composed of Members chosen every second Year by the People of the several States, and the Electors in each State shall have the Qualifications requisite for Electors of the most numerous Branch of the State Legislature.
>
> Representatives and direct Taxes shall be apportioned among the several States which may be included within this Union according to their respective Numbers, which shall be determined by adding to the whole Number of free Persons, including those bound to Service for a Term of Years, and excluding Indians not taxed, three fifths of all other Persons. The actual Enumeration shall be made within three Years after the first Meeting of the Congress of the United States, and within every subsequent Term of ten Years, in such Manner

as they shall by Law direct. The Number of Representatives shall not exceed one for every thirty Thousand, but each State shall have at Least one Representative . . .

Section 4. The Times, Places and Manner of holding Elections for Senators and Representatives, shall be prescribed in each State by the Legislature thereof; but the Congress may at any time by Law make or alter such Regulations, except as to the Places of chusing Senators.

Section 5. Each House shall be the Judge of the Elections, Returns and Qualifications of its own Members. . . .

As will be shown, these constitutional provisions and their "historical context," establish:

1. that congressional Representatives are to be apportioned among the several States largely, but not entirely, according to population;

2. that the States have plenary power to select their allotted Representatives in accordance with any method of popular election they please, subject only to the supervisory power of Congress; and

3. that the supervisory power of Congress is exclusive.

In short, in the absence of legislation providing for equal listricts by the Georgia Legislature or by Congress, these ippellants have no right to the judicial relief which they eek. It goes without saying that it is beyond the province of this Court to decide whether equally populated districts s the preferable method for electing Representatives, vhether state legislatures would have acted more fairly or visely had they adopted such a method, or whether Congress has been derelict in not requiring state legislatures to ollow that course. Once it is clear that there is no *contitutional* right at stake, that ends the case. . . .

[There follows a lengthy analysis of the debates in the Constitutional Convention and the state ratifying conventions concerning the relevant sections cited.]

The upshot of all this is that the language of Art. I, § 2 nd § 4, the surrounding text, and the relevant history are ll in strong and consistent direct contradiction of the Court's holding. The constitutional scheme vests in the tates plenary power to regulate the conduct of elections or Representatives, and, in order to protect the Federal Government, provides for congressional supervision of the tates' exercise of their power. Within this scheme, the apellants do not have the right which they assert, in the abence of provision for equal districts by the Georgia Legislature or the Congress. The constitutional right which the Court creates is manufactured out of whole cloth.

The unstated premise of the Court's conclusion quite obviously is that the Congress has not dealt, and the Court believes it will not deal, with the problem of congressional apportionment in accordance with what the Court believes to be sound political principles. Laying aside for the moment the validity of such a consideration as a factor in constitutional interpretation, it becomes relevant to examine the history of congressional action under Art. I, § 4. This history reveals that the Court is not simply undertaking to exercise a power which the Constitution reserves to the Congress; it is also overruling congressional judgment.

Congress exercised its power to regulate elections for the House of Representatives for the first time in 1842, when it provided that Representatives from States "entitled to more than one Representative" should be elected by districts of contiguous territory, "no one district electing more than one Representative." The requirement was later dropped and reinstated. In 1872, Congress required that Representatives "be elected by districts composed of contiguous territory, and containing as nearly as practicable an equal number of inhabitants, . . . no one district electing more than one Representative." This provision for equal districts which the Court exactly duplicates in effect, was carried forward in each subsequent apportionment statute through 1911. There was no reapportionment following the 1920 census. The provision for equally populated districts was dropped in 1929, and has not been revived, although the 1929 provisions for apportionment have twice been amended and, in 1941, were made generally applicable to subsequent censuses and apportionments. . . .

Today's decision has portents for our society and the Court itself which should be recognized. This is not a case in which the Court vindicates the kind of individual rights that are assured by the Due Process Clause of the Fourteenth Amendment, whose "vague contours," *Rochin v. California*, 342 U.S. 165, 170, of course leave much room for constitutional developments necessitated by changing conditions in a dynamic society. Nor is this a case in which an emergent set of facts requires the Court to frame new principles to protect recognized constitutional rights. The claim for judicial relief in this case strikes at one of the fundamental doctrines of our system of government, the sep aration of powers. In upholding that claim, the Court attempts to effect reforms in a field which the Constitution, as plainly as can be, has committed exclusively to the political process.

This Court, no less than all other branches of the Government, is bound by the Constitution. The Constitution does not confer on the Court blanket authority to step into every situation where the political branch may be thought to have fallen short. The stability of this institution ultimately depends not only upon its being alert to keep the other branches of government within constitutional bounds but equally upon recognition of the limitations on the Court's own functions in the constitutional system.

What is done today saps the political process. The promise of judicial intervention in matters of this sort cannot but encourage popular inertia in efforts for political reform through the political process, with the inevitable result that the process is itself weakened. By yielding to the demand for a judicial remedy in this instance, the Court in my view does a disservice both to itself and to the broader values of our system of government.

Believing that the complaint fails to disclose a constitutional claim, I would affirm the judgment below dismissing the complaint.

MR. JUSTICE STEWART.

I think it is established that "this Court has power to afford relief in a case of this type as against the objection that the issues are not justiciable," * and I cannot subscribe to any possible implication to the contrary which may lurk in MR. JUSTICE HARLAN'S dissenting opinion. With this single qualification I join the dissent because I think MR. JUSTICE HARLAN has unanswerably demonstrated that Art. I, § 2, of the Constitution gives no mandate to this Court or to any court to ordain that congressional districts within each State must be equal in population.

* The quotation is from Mr. Justice Rutledge's concurring opinion in *Colegrove v. Green*, 328 U.S., at 565.

Reynolds v. Sims (377 U.S. 533)
Decided June 15, 1964

MR. CHIEF JUSTICE WARREN *delivered the opinion of the Court.*

Involved in these cases are an appeal and two cross-appeals from a decision of the Federal District Court for the Middle District of Alabama holding invalid, under the Equal Protection Clause of the Federal Constitution, the existing and two legislatively proposed plans for the apportionment of seats in the two houses of the Alabama Legislature, and ordering into effect a temporary reapportionment plan comprised of parts of the proposed but judicially disapproved measures. . . .

In *Baker v. Carr*, 369 U.S. 186, we held that a claim asserted under the Equal Protection Clause challenging the constitutionality of a State's apportionment of seats in its legislature, on the ground that the right to vote of certain citizens was effectively impaired since debased and diluted in effect, presented a justiciable controversy subject to adjudication by federal courts. The spate of similar cases filed and decided by lower courts since our decision in *Baker* amply shows that the problem of state legislative malapportionment is one that is perceived to exist in a large number of the States. . . .

In *Gray v. Sanders*, 372 U.S. 368, we held that the Georgia county unit system, applicable in statewide primary elections, was unconstitutional since it resulted in a dilution of the weight of the votes of certain Georgia voters merely because of where they resided. . . .

In *Wesberry v. Sanders*, 376 U.S. 1, decided earlier this Term, we held that attacks on the constitutionality of congressional districting plans enacted by state legislatures do not present nonjusticiable questions and should not be dismissed generally for "want of equity." We determined that the constitutional test for the validity of congressional districting schemes was one of substantial equality of population among the various districts established by a state legislature for the election of members of the federal house of representatives.

. . . *Wesberry* clearly established that the fundamental principle of representative government in this country is one of equal representation for equal numbers of people, without regard to race, sex, economic status, or place of residence within a state. Our problem, then, is to ascertain, in the instant cases, whether there are any constitutionally cognizable principles which would justify departures from the basic standard of equality among voters in the apportionment of seats in state legislatures.

A predominant consideration in determining whether a State's legislative apportionment scheme constitutes an invidious discrimination violative of rights asserted under the Equal Protection Clause is that the rights allegedly impaired are individual and personal in nature. As stated by the Court in *United States v. Bathgate*, 246 U.S. 220, 227, "[t]he right to vote is personal. . . ." While the result of a court decision in a state legislative apportionment controversy may be to require the restructuring of the geographical distribution of seats in a state legislature, the judicial focus must be concentrated upon ascertaining whether there has been any discrimination against certain of the State's citizens which constitutes an impermissible impairment of their constitutionally protected right to vote. Like *Skinner v. Oklahoma*, 316 U.S. 535, such a case "touches a sensitive and important area of human rights," and "involves one of the basic civil rights of man," presenting questions of alleged "invidious discriminations . . . against groups or types of individuals in violation of the constitutional guaranty of just and equal laws," 316 U.S., at 536, 541. Undoubtedly, the right of suffrage is a fundamental matter in a free and democratic society. Especially since the right to exercise the franchise in a free and unimpaired manner is preservative of other basic civil and political rights, any alleged infringement of the right of citizens to vote must be carefully and meticulously scrutinized.

Legislators represent people, not trees or acres. Legislators are elected by voters, not farms or cities or economic interests. As long as ours is a representative form of government, and our legislatures are those instruments of government elected directly by and directly representative of the people, the right to elect legislators in a free and unimpaired fashion is a bedrock of our political system. . . . And, if a State should provide that the votes of citizens in one part of the State should be given two times, or five times, or ten times the weight of votes of citizens in another part of the State, it could hardly be contended that the right to vote of those residing in the disfavored areas had not been effectively diluted. It would appear extraordinary to suggest that a State could be constitutionally permitted to enact a law providing that certain of the State's voters could vote two, five, or ten times for their legislative representatives, while voters living elsewhere could vote only once. And it is inconceivable that a state law to the effect that, in counting votes for legislators, the votes of citizens in one part of the State would be multiplied by two, five, or ten, while the votes of persons in another area would be counted only at face value, could be constitutionally sustainable. . . . Weighting the votes of citizens differently, by any method or means, merely because of where they happen to reside, hardly seems justifiable. One must be ever aware that the Constitution forbids "sophisticated as well as simple-minded modes of discrimination." *Lane v. Wilson*, 307 U.S. 268, 275, *Gomillion v. Lightfoot*, 364 U.S. 339, 342. . . .

Logically, in a society ostensibly grounded on representative government, it would seem reasonable that a majority of the people of a State could elect a majority of that State's legislators. To conclude differently, and to sanction minority control of state legislative bodies, would appear to deny majority rights in a way that far surpasses any possible denial of minority rights that might otherwise be thought to result. Since legislatures are responsible for enacting laws by which all citizens are to be governed, they should be bodies which are collectively responsive to the popular will. And the concept of equal protection has been traditionally viewed as requiring the uniform treatment of persons standing in the same relation to the governmental action questioned or challenged. With respect to the allocation of legislative representation, all voters, as citizens of a State, stand in the same relation regardless of where they live. Any suggested criteria for the differentiation of citizens are insufficient to justify any discrimination, as to the weight of their votes, unless relevant to the permissible purposes of legislative apportionment. Since the achieving of fair and effective representation for all citizens is concededly the basic aim of legislative apportionment, we conclude that the Equal Protection Clause guarantees the opportunity for equal participation by all voters in the election of state legislators. . . . Our constitutional system amply provides for the protection of minorities by means other than giving them majority control of state legislatures. And the democratic ideals of equality and majority rule, which have served this Nation so well in the past, are hardly of any less significance for the present and the future.

We are told that the matter of apportioning representation in a state legislature is a complex and many-faceted one. We are advised that States can rationally consider factors other than population in apportioning legislative representation. We are admonished not to restrict the power of the States to impose differing views as to political philosophy on their citizens. We are cautioned about the dangers of entering into political thickets and mathematical quagmires. Our answer is this: a denial of constitutionally protected rights demands judicial protection; our oath and our office require no less of us. As stated in *Gomillion v. Lightfoot, supra:* "When a State exercises power wholly within the domain of state interest, it is insulated from federal judicial review. But such insulation is not carried over when state power is used as an instrument for circumventing a federally protected right." To the extent that a citizen's right to vote is debased, he is that much less a citizen. The fact that an individual lives here or there is not a legitimate reason for overweighting or diluting the efficacy of his vote. The complexions of societies and civilizations change, often with amazing rapidity. A nation once primarily rural in character becomes predominantly urban. Representation schemes once fair and equitable become archaic and outdated. But the basic principle of representative government remains, and must remain, unchanged—the weight of a citizen's vote cannot be made to depend on where he lives. Population is, of necessity, the starting point for consideration and the controlling criterion for judgment in legislative apportionment controversies. . . .

IV.

We hold that, as a basic constitutional standard, the Equal Protection Clause requires that the seats in both houses of a bicameral state legislature must be apportioned on a population basis. Simply stated, an individual's right to vote for state legislators is unconstitutionally impaired when its weight is in a substantial fashion diluted when compared with votes of citizens living in other parts of the State. Since, under neither the existing apportionment provisions nor under either of the proposed plans was either of the houses of the Alabama Legislature apportioned on a population basis, the District Court correctly held that all three of these schemes were constitutionally invalid. . . .

V.

Since neither of the houses of the Alabama Legislature, under any of the three plans considered by the District Court, was apportioned on a population basis, we would be justified in proceeding no further. However, one of the proposed plans, that contained in the so-called 67-Senator Amendment, at least superficially resembles the scheme of legislative representation followed in the Federal Congress. Under this plan, each of Alabama's 67 counties is allotted one senator, and no counties are given more than one senate seat. Arguably, this is analogous to the allocation of two senate seats, in the Federal Congress, to each of the 50 States, regardless of population. Seats in the Alabama House, under the proposed constitutional amendment, are distributed by giving each of the 67 counties at least one, with the remaining 39 seats being allotted among the more populous counties on a population basis. This scheme, at least at first glance, appears to resemble that prescribed for the Federal house of representatives, where the 435 seats are distributed among the States on a population basis, although each State, regardless of its population, is given at least one congressman. Thus, although there are substantial differences in underlying rationale and result, the 67-Senator Amendment, as proposed by the Alabama Legislature, at least arguably presents for consideration a scheme analogous to that used for apportioning seats in Congress.

Much has been written since our decision in *Baker v. Carr* about the applicability of the so-called federal analogy to state legislative apportionment arrangements. . . . We find the federal analogy inapposite and irrelevant to state legislative districting schemes. Attempted reliance on the federal analogy appears often to be little more than an after-the-fact rationalization offered in defense of maladjusted state apportionment arrangements. The original constitutions of 36 of our states provided that representation in both houses of the state legislatures would be based completely, or predominantly, on population. And the Founding Fathers clearly had no intention of establishing a pattern or model for the apportionment of seats in state legislatures when the system of representation in the Federal Congress was adopted. Demonstrative of this is the fact that the Northwest Ordinance, adopted in the same year, 1787, as the Federal Constitution, provided for the apportionment of seats in territorial legislatures solely on the basis of population.

The system of representation in the two Houses of the Federal Congress is one ingrained in our Constitution, as part of the law of the land. It is one conceived out of compromise and concession indispensable to the establishment of our federal republic. Arising from unique historical circumstances, it is based on the consideration that in establishing our type of federalism a group of formerly independent States bound themselves together under one national government. Admittedly, the original 13 States surrendered some of their sovereignty in agreeing to join together "to form a more perfect Union." But at the heart of our constitutional system remains the concept of separate and distinct governmental entities which have delegated some, but not all, of their formerly held powers to the single national government. . . .

Political subdivisions of States—counties, cities, or whatever—never were and never have been considered as sovereign entities. Rather, they have been traditionally regarded as subordinate governmental instrumentalities created by the State to assist in the carrying out of state governmental functions. As stated by the Court in *Hunter v. City of Pittsburgh*, 207 U.S. 161, 178, these governmental units are "created as convenient agencies for exercising such of the governmental powers of the state as may be entrusted to them" and the "number, nature, and duration of the powers conferred upon [them] . . . and the territory over which they shall be exercised rests in the absolute discretion of the state." The relationship of the states to the Federal government could hardly be less analogous. . . .

Since we find the so-called federal analogy inapposite to a consideration of the constitutional validity of state legislative apportionment schemes, we necessarily hold that the Equal Protection Clause requires both houses of a state legislature to be apportioned on a population basis. The right of a citizen to equal representation and to have his vote weighted equally with those of all other citizens in the election of members of one house of a bicameral state legislature would amount to little if States could effectively submerge the equal-population principle in the apportionment of seats in the other house. If such a scheme were permissible, an individual citizen's ability to exercise an effective voice in the only instrument of state government directly representative of the people might be almost as effectively thwarted as if neither house were apportioned on a population basis. Deadlock between the two bodies might result in compromise and concession on some issues. But in all too many cases the more probable result would be frustration of the majority will through minority veto in the house not apportioned on a population basis, stemming directly from the failure to accord adequate overall legislative representation to all of the state's citizens on a nondiscriminatory basis. In summary, we can perceive no constitutional difference, with respect to the geographical distribution of state legislative representation, between the two houses of a bicameral state legislature.

We do not believe that the concept of bicameralism is rendered anachronistic and meaningless when the predominant basis of representation in the two state legislative bodies is required to be the same—population. A prime reason for bicameralism, modernly considered, is to insure mature and deliberate consideration of, and to prevent precipitate action on, proposed legislative measures. Simply because the controlling criterion for apportioning representation is required to be the same in both houses does not mean that there will be no differences in the composition and complexion of the two bodies. Different constituencies can be represented in the two houses. One body could be composed of single-member districts while the other could have at least some multimember districts. The length of terms of the legislators in the separate bodies could differ. The numerical size of the two bodies could be made to differ, even significantly, and the geographical size of districts from which legislators are elected could also be made to differ. And apportionment in one house could be arranged so as to balance off minor inequities in the representation of certain areas in the other house. In summary, these and other factors could be, and are presently in many States, utilized to engender differing complexions and collective attitudes in the two bodies of a state legislature, although both are apportioned substantially on a population basis.

VI.

By holding that as a federal constitutional requisite both houses of a state legislature must be apportioned on a population basis, we mean that the Equal Protection Clause requires that a State make an honest and good faith effort to construct districts, in both houses of its legislature, as nearly of equal population as is practicable. We realize that it is a practical impossibility to arrange legislative districts so that each one has an identical number of residents, or citizens, or voters. Mathematical exactness or precision is hardly a workable constitutional requirement.

. . . Lower courts can and assuredly will work out more concrete and specific standards for evaluating state legislative apportionment schemes in the context of actual litigation. For the present, we deem it expedient not to attempt to spell out any precise constitutional tests. What is marginally permissible in one State may be unsatisfactory in another, depending on the particular circumstances of the case. Developing a body of doctrine on a case-by-case basis appears to us to provide the most satisfactory means of arriving at detailed constitutional requirements in the area of state legislative apportionment. Thus, we proceed to state here only a few rather general considerations which appear to us to be relevant.

A State may legitimately desire to maintain the integrity of various political subdivisions, insofar as possible, and provide for compact districts of contiguous territory in designing a legislative apportionment scheme. Valid considerations may underlie such aims. Indiscriminate districting, without any regard for political subdivision or natural or historical boundary lines, may be little more than an open invitation to partisan gerrymandering. Single-member districts may be the rule in one state, while another state might desire to achieve some flexibility by creating multimember or floterial districts. Whatever the means of accomplishment, the overriding objective must be substantial equality of population among the various districts, so that the vote of any citizen is approximately equal in weight to that of any other citizen in the State.

History indicates, however, that many States have deviated, to a greater or lesser degree, from the equal-population principle in the apportionment of seats in at least one house of their legislatures. So long as the divergences from a strict population standard are based on legitimate considerations incident to the effectuation of a rational state policy, some deviations from the equal-population principle are constitutionally permissible with respect to the apportionment of seats in either or both of the two houses of a bicameral state legislature. But neither history alone, nor economic or other sorts of group interests, are permissible factors in attempting to justify disparities from population-based representation. Citizens, not history or economic interest, cast votes. Considerations of area alone provide an insufficient justification for deviations from the equal-population principle. Again, people, not land or trees or pastures, vote. Modern developments and improvements in transportation and communications make rather hollow, in the mid-1960's, most claims that deviations from population-based representation can validly be based solely on geographical considerations. Arguments for allowing such deviations in order to insure effective representation for sparsely settled areas and to prevent legislative districts from becoming so large that the availability of access of citizens to their representatives is impaired are today, for the most part, unconvincing. . . .

VIII.

That the Equal Protection Clause requires that both houses of a state legislature be apportioned on a population basis does not mean that States cannot adopt some reasonable plan for periodic revision of their apportionment schemes. Decennial reapportionment appears to be a rational approach to readjustment of legislative representation in order to take into account population shifts and growth. Reallocation of legislative seats every ten years coincides with the prescribed practice in 41 of the States, often honored more in the breach than the observance, however. . . . [W]e do not mean to intimate that more frequent reapportionment would not be constitutionally permissible or practically desirable. But if reapportionment were accomplished with less frequency, it would assuredly be constitutionally suspect. . . .

X.

We do not consider here the difficult question of the proper remedial devices which federal courts should utilize in state legislative apportionment cases. Remedial technique in this new and developing area of the law will probably often differ with the circumstances of the challenged apportionment and a variety of local conditions. It is enough to say now that, once a state's legislative apportionment scheme has been found to be unconstitutional, it would be the unusual case in which a court would be justified in not taking appropriate action to insure that no further elections are conducted under the invalid plan. However, under certain circumstances, such as where an impending election is imminent and a State's election machinery is already in progress, equitable considerations might justify a court in withholding the granting of immediately effective relief in a legislative apportionment case, even though the existing apportionment scheme was found invalid. In awarding or withholding immediate relief, a court is entitled to and should consider the proximity of a forthcoming election and the mechanics and complexities of state election laws, and should act and rely upon general equitable principles.

MR. JUSTICE HARLAN, *dissenting.*

In these cases the Court holds that seats in the legislatures of six States are apportioned in ways that violate the Federal Constitution. Under the Court's ruling it is bound to follow that the legislatures in all but a few of the other 44 States will meet the same fate. These decisions, with *Wesberry v. Sanders,* 376 U.S. 1, involving congressional districting by the States, and *Gray v. Sanders,* 372 U.S. 368, relating to elections for statewide office, have the effect of placing basic aspects of state political systems under the pervasive overlordship of the federal judiciary. Once again, I must register my protest. . . .

With these cases the Court approaches the end of the third round set in motion by the complaint filed in *Baker v. Carr.* What is done today deepens my conviction that judicial entry into this realm is profoundly ill-advised and constitutionally impermissible. As I have said before, *Wesberry v. Sanders, supra,* at 48, I believe that the vitality of our political system, on which in the last analysis all else depends, is weakened by reliance on the judiciary for political reform; in time a complacent body politic may result.

These decisions also cut deeply into the fabric of our federalism. What must follow from them may eventually appear to be the product of State Legislatures. Nevertheless, no thinking person can fail to recognize that the aftermath of these cases, however desirable it may be thought in itself, will have been achieved at the cost of a radical alteration in the relationship between the States and the Federal Government, more particularly the Federal Judiciary. Only one who has an overbearing impatience with the federal system and its political processes will believe that that cost was not too high or was inevitable.

Finally, these decisions give support to a current mistaken view of the Constitution and the constitutional function of this Court. This view, in a nutshell, is that every major social ill in this country can find its cure in some constitutional "principle," and that this Court should "take the lead" in promoting reform when other branches of government fail to act. The Constitution is not a panacea for every blot upon the public welfare, nor should this Court, ordained as a judicial body, be thought of as a general haven for reform movements. The Constitution is an instrument of government, fundamental to which is the premise that in a diffusion of governmental authority lies the greatest promise that this Nation will realize liberty for all its citizens. This Court, limited in function in accordance with that premise, does not serve its high purpose when it exceeds its authority, even to satisfy justified impatience with the slow workings of the political process. For when, in the name of constitutional interpretation, the Court *adds* something to the Constitution that was deliberately excluded from it, the Court in reality substitutes its view of what should be so for the amending process.

I dissent in each of these cases, believing that in none of them have the plaintiffs stated a cause of action. To the extent that *Baker v. Carr*, expressly or by implication, went beyond a discussion of jurisdictional doctrines independent of the substantive issues involved here, it should be limited to what it in fact was: an experiment in venturesome constitutionalism.

Lucas v. 44th General Assembly of Colorado (377 U.S. 713)
Decided June 15, 1964

MR. CHIEF JUSTICE WARREN *delivered the opinion of the Court.*

At the November 1962 general election, the Colorado electorate adopted proposed Amendment No. 7 by a vote of 305,700 to 172,725, and defeated proposed Amendment No. 8 by a vote of 311,749 to 149,822. Amendment No. 8, rejected by a majority of the voters, prescribed an apportionment plan pursuant to which seats in both houses of the Colorado Legislature would purportedly be apportioned on a population basis. Amendment No. 7, on the other hand, provided for the apportionment of the House of Representatives on the basis of population, but essentially maintained the existing apportionment in the Senate, which was based on a combination of population and various other factors. Plaintiffs below requested a declaration that Amendment No. 7 was unconstitutional under the Fourteenth Amendment since resulting in substantial disparities from population-based representation in the Senate, and asked for a decree reapportioning both houses of the Colorado Legislature on a population basis. . . .

Several aspects of this case serve to distinguish it from the other cases involving state legislative apportionment also decided this date. Initially, one house of the Colorado Legislature is at least arguably apportioned substantially on a population basis under Amendment No. 7 and the implementing statutory provisions. Under the apportionment schemes challenged in the other cases, on the other hand, clearly neither of the houses in any of the State legislatures is apportioned sufficiently on a population basis so as to be constitutionally sustainable. Additionally, the Colorado scheme of legislative apportionment here attacked is one adopted by a majority vote of the Colorado electorate almost contemporaneously with the District Court's decision on the merits in this litigation. Thus, the plan at issue did not result from prolonged legislative inaction. However, the Colorado General Assembly, in spite of the state constitutional mandate for periodic reapportionment, has enacted only one effective legislative apportionment measure in the past fifty years.

Finally, this case differs from the others decided this date in that the initiative device provides a practicable political remedy to obtain relief against alleged legislative malapportionment in Colorado. An initiated measure proposing a constitutional amendment or a statutory enactment is entitled to be placed on the ballot if the signatures of 8 percent of those voting for the secretary of state in the last election are obtained.

Except as an interim remedial procedure justifying a court in staying its hand temporarily, we find no significance in the fact that a nonjudicial, political remedy may be available for the effectuation of asserted rights to equal representation in a state legislature. Courts sit to adjudicate controversies involving alleged denials of constitutional rights. While a court sitting as a court of equity might be justified in temporarily refraining from the issuance of injunctive relief in an apportionment case in order to allow for resort to an available political remedy, such as initiative and referendum, individual constitutional rights cannot be deprived, or denied judicial effectuation, because of the existence of a nonjudicial remedy through which relief against the alleged malapportionment, which the individual voters seek, might be achieved. An individual's constitutionally protected right to cast an equally weighted vote cannot be denied even by a vote of a majority of a state's electorate, if the apportionment scheme adopted by the voters fails to measure up to the requirements of the Equal Protection Clause. Manifestly, the fact that an apportionment plan is adopted in a popular referendum is insufficient to sustain its constitutionality or to induce a court of equity to refuse to act. As stated by this Court in *West Virginia State Bd. of Educ. v. Barnette*, 319 U.S. 624, 638, "One's right to life, liberty, and property . . . and the other fundamental rights may not be submitted to vote; they depend on the outcome of no elections." A citizen's constitutional rights can hardly be infringed simply because a majority of the people choose to do so. We hold that the fact that a challenged legislative apportionment plan was approved by the electorate is without federal constitutional significance, if the scheme adopted fails to satisfy the basic requirements of the Equal Protection Clause, as delineated in our opinion in *Reynolds v. Sims*. And we conclude that the fact that a practicably available political remedy, such as initiative and referendum, exists under state law provides justification only for a court of equity to stay its hand temporarily while recourse to such a remedial device is attempted or while proposed initiated measures relating to legislative apportionment are pending and will be submitted to the State's voters at the next election. . . .

MR. JUSTICE STEWART, *whom* MR. JUSTICE CLARK *joins, dissenting.*

It is important to make clear at the outset what these cases are not about. They have nothing to do with the denial or impairment of any person's right to vote. Nobody's right to vote has been denied. Nobody's right to vote has been restricted. Nobody has been deprived of the right to have his vote counted. The voting right cases which the Court cites are, therefore, completely wide of the mark. Secondly, these cases have nothing to do with the "weighting" or "diluting" of votes cast within any electoral unit. The rule of *Gray v. Sanders*, 372 U.S. 368, is, therefore, completely without relevance here. Thirdly, these cases are not concerned with the election of members of the Congress of the United States, governed by Article I of the Constitution. Consequently, the Court's decision in *Wesberry v. Sanders*, 376 U.S. 1, throws no light at all on the basic issue now before us.

The question involved in these cases is quite a different one. Simply stated, the question is to what degree, if at all, the Equal Protection Clause of the Fourteenth Amendment limits each sovereign State's freedom to establish appropriate electoral constituencies from which representatives to the State's bicameral legislative assembly are to be chosen. The Court's answer is a blunt one, and, I think, woefully wrong. The Equal Protection Clause, says the Court, "requires that the seats in both houses of a bicameral state legislature must be apportioned on a population basis."

After searching carefully through the Court's opinions in these and their companion cases, I have been able to find but two reasons offered in support of this rule. First, says the Court, it is "established that the fundamental principle of representative government in this country is one of equal representation for equal numbers of people. . . ." With all respect, I think that this is not correct, simply as a matter of fact. . . . Secondly, says the Court, unless legislative districts are equal in population, voters in the more populous districts will suffer a "debasement" amounting to a constitutional injury. As the Court explains it, "To the extent that a citizen's right to vote is debased, he is that much less a citizen." We are not told how or why the vote of a person in a more populated legislative district is "debased," or how or why he is less a citizen, nor is the proposition self-evident. . . .

To put the matter plainly, there is nothing in all the history of this Court's decisions which supports this constitutional rule. The Court's draconian pronouncement, which makes unconstitutional the legislatures of most of the 50 States, finds no support in the words of the Constitution, in any prior decision of this Court, or in the 175-year political history of our Federal Union. With all respect, I am convinced these decisions mark a long step backward into that unhappy era when a majority of the members of this Court were thought by many to have convinced themselves and each other that the demands of the Constitution were to be measured not by what it says, but by their notions of wise political theory. The rule announced today is at odds with long-established principles of constitutional adjudication under the Equal Protection Clause, and it stifles values of local individuality and initiative vital to the character of the Federal Union which it was the genius of our Constitution to create.

I.

What the Court has done is to convert a particular political philosophy into a constitutional rule, binding upon each of the 50 States, from Maine to Hawaii, from Alaska to Texas, without regard and without respect for the many individualized and differentiated characteristics of each State, characteristics stemming from each State's distinct history, distinct geography, distinct distribution of population, and distinct political heritage. My own understanding of the various theories of representative government is that no one theory has ever commanded unanimous assent among political scientists, historians, or others who have considered the problem. But even if it were thought that the rule announced today by the Court is, as a matter of political theory, the most desirable general rule which can be devised as a basis for the make-up of the representative assembly of a typical State, I could not join in the fabrication of a constitutional mandate which imports and forever freezes one theory of political thought into our Constitution, and forever denies to every State any opportunity for enlightened and progressive innovation in the design of its democratic institutions, so as to accommodate within a system of representative government the interests and aspirations of diverse groups of people, without subjecting any group or class to absolute domination by a geographically concentrated or highly organized majority.

Representative government is a process of accommodating group interests through democratic institutional arrangements. Its function is to channel the numerous opinions, interests, and abilities of the people of a State into the making of the State's public policy. Appropriate legislative apportionment, therefore, should ideally be designed to insure effective representation in the State's legislature, in cooperation with other organs of political power, of the various groups and interests making up the electorate. In practice, of course, this ideal is approximated in the particular apportionment system of any State by a realistic accommodation of the diverse and often conflicting political forces operating within the State.

I do not pretend to any specialized knowledge of the myriad of individual characteristics of the several States, beyond the records in the cases before us today. But I do know enough to be aware that a system of legislative apportionment which might be best for South Dakota, might be unwise for Hawaii with its many islands, or Michigan with its Northern Peninsula. I do know enough to realize that Montana with its vast distances is not Rhode Island with its heavy concentrations of people. I do know enough to be aware of the great variations among the several States in their historic manner of disturbing legislative power—of the Governors' Councils in New England, of the broad powers of initiative and referendum retained in some States by the people, of the legislative power which some States give to their Governors, by the right of veto or otherwise, of the widely autonomous home rule which many States give to their cities. The Court today declines to give any recognition to these considerations and countless others, tangible and intangible, in holding unconstitutional the particular systems of legislative apportionment which these States have chosen. Instead, the Court says that the requirements of the Equal Protection Clause can be met in any State only by the uncritical, simplistic, and heavy-handed application of sixth-grade arithmetic.

But legislators do not represent faceless numbers. They represent people, or, more accurately, a majority of the voters in their districts—people with identifiable needs and interests which require legislative representation, and which can often be related to the geographical areas in which these people live. The very fact of geographic districting, the constitutional validity of which the Court does not question, carries with it an acceptance of the idea of legislative representation of regional needs and interests. Yet if geographical residence is irrelevant, as the Court suggests, and the goal is solely that of equally "weighted" votes, I do not understand why the Court's constitutional rule does not require the abolition of districts and the holding of all elections at large.

The fact is, of course, that population factors must often to some degree be subordinated in devising a legislative apportionment plan which is to achieve the important goal of ensuring a fair, effective, and balanced representation of the regional, social, and economic interests within a State. And the further fact is that throughout our history the apportionments of State Legislatures have reflected the strongly felt American tradition that the public interest is composed of many diverse interests, and that in the long run it can better be expressed by a medley of component voices than by the majority's monolithic command. What constitutes a rational plan reasonably designed to achieve this objective will vary from State to State, since each State is unique, in terms of topography, geography, demography, history, heterogeneity and concentration of population, variety of social and economic interests, and in the operation and interrelation of its political institutions. But so long as a State's apportionment plan reasonably achieves, in the light of the State's own characteristics, effective and balanced representation of all substantial interests, without sacrificing the principle of effective majority rule, that plan cannot be considered irrational.

II.

This brings me to what I consider to be the proper constitutional standards to be applied in these cases. Quite simply, I think the cases should be decided by application of accepted principles of constitutional adjudication under the Equal Protection Clause. . . .

Moving from the general to the specific, I think that the Equal Protection Clause demands but two basic attributes of any plan of state legislative apportionment. First, it demands that, in the light of the State's own characteristics and needs, the plan must be a rational one. Secondly, it demands that the plan must be such as not to permit the systematic frustration of the will of a majority of the electorate of the State. I think it is apparent that any plan of legislative apportionment which could be shown to reflect no policy, but simply arbitrary and capricious action or inaction, and that any plan which could be shown systematically to prevent ultimate effective majority rule, would be invalid under accepted Equal Protection Clause standards. But, beyond this, I think there is nothing in the Federal Constitution to prevent a State from choosing any electoral legislative structure it thinks best suited to the interests, temper, and customs of its people. . . .

III.

Colorado.

The Colorado plan creates a General Assembly composed of a Senate of 39 members and a House of 65 members. The State is divided into 65 equal population representative districts, with one representative to be elected from each district, and 39 senatorial districts, 14 of which include more than one county. In the Colorado House, the majority unquestionably rules supreme, with the population factor untempered by other considerations. In the Senate rural minorities do not have effective control, and therefore do not have even a veto power over the will of the urban majorities. It is true that, as a matter of theoretical arithmetic, a minority of 36 percent of the voters could elect a majority of the Senate, but this percentage has no real meaning in terms of the legislative process. Under the Colorado plan, no possible combination of Colorado senators from rural districts, even assuming *arguendo* that they would vote as a bloc, could control the Senate. To arrive at the 36 percent figure, one must include with the rural districts a substantial number of urban districts, districts with substantially dissimilar interests. There is absolutely no reason to assume that this theoretical majority would ever vote together on any issue so as to thwart the wishes of the majority of the voters of Colorado. Indeed, when we eschew the world of numbers, and look to the real world of effective representation, the simple fact of the matter is that Colorado's three metropolitan areas, Denver, Pueblo, and Colorado Springs, elect a majority of the Senate.

It is clear from the record that if per capita representation were the rule in both houses of the Colorado Legislature, counties having small populations would have to be merged with larger counties having totally dissimilar interests. Their representatives would not only be unfamiliar with the problems of the smaller county, but the interests of the smaller counties might well be totally submerged to the interests of the larger counties with which they are joined. Since representatives representing conflicting interests might well pay greater attention to the views of the majority, the minority interest could be denied any effective representation at all. Its votes would not be merely "diluted," an injury which the Court considers of constitutional dimensions, but rendered totally nugatory.

The findings of the District Court speak for themselves:

> The heterogeneous characteristics of Colorado justify geographic districting for the election of the members of one chamber of the legislature. In no other way may representation be afforded to insular minorities. Without such districting the metropolitan areas could theoretically, and no doubt practically, dominate both chambers of the legislature.
>
> . . . The realities of topographic conditions with their resulting effect on population may not be ignored. For an example, if [the rule of equal population districts] was to be accepted, Colorado would have one senator for approximately every 45,000 persons. Two contiguous Western Region senatorial districts, Nos. 29 and 37, have a combined population of 51,675 persons inhabiting an area of 20,514 square miles. The division of this area into two districts does not offend any constitutional provisions. Rather, it is a wise recognition of the practicalities of life. . . .
>
> We are convinced that the apportionment of the Senate by Amendment No. 7 recognizes population as a prime, but not

> controlling, factor and gives effect to such important considerations as geography, compactness and contiguity of territory, accessibility, observance of natural boundaries, conformity to historical divisions such as county lines and prior representation districts, and "a proper diffusion of political initiative as between a state's thinly populated counties and those having concentrated masses."
>
> 219 F. Supp., at 932.

From 1954 until the adoption of Amendment 7 in 1962, the issue of apportionment had been the subject of intense public debate. The present apportionment was proposed and supported by many of Colorado's leading citizens. The factual data underlying the apportionment were prepared by the wholly independent Denver Research Institute of the University of Denver. Finally, the apportionment was adopted by a popular referendum in which not only a 2-1 majority of all the voters in Colorado, but a majority in each county, including those urban counties allegedly discriminated against, voted for the present plan in preference to an alternative proposal providing for equal representation per capita in both legislative houses. As the District Court said:

> The contention that the voters have discriminated against themselves appalls rather than convinces. Difficult as it may be at times to understand mass behavior of human beings, a proper recognition of the judicial function precludes a court from holding that the free choice of the voters between two conflicting theories of apportionment is irrational or the result arbitrary. *Ibid.*

The present apportionment, adopted overwhelmingly by the people in a 1962 popular referendum as a state constitutional amendment, is entirely rational, and the amendment by its terms provides for keeping the apportionment current. Thus the majority has consciously chosen to protect the minority's interests, and under the liberal initiative provisions of the Colorado Constitution, it retains the power to reverse its decision to do so. Therefore, there can be no question of frustration of the basic principle of majority rule.

INDEX